Blenheim Revisited

BLENHEIM REVISITED

The Spencer-Churchills and their Palace

HUGH MONTGOMERY-MASSINGBERD

BEAUFORT BOOKS
Publishers
NEW YORK

Produced, designed and edited by
Shuckburgh Reynolds Limited,
289 Westbourne Grove, London W11 2QA.

Designer: Behram Kapadia

Library of Congress Cataloging in Publication Data
Montgomery-Massingberd, Hugh.
  Blenheim revisited.

  1. Blenheim Palace (Blenheim, Oxfordshire)
2. Blenheim (Oxfordshire) – Palaces.   3. Churchill family.
4. Spencer family.   I. Title.
DA690.B635M66 1984   942.5'71   85-1221
  ISBN 0-8253-0297-8

Published in the United States by Beaufort Books
  Publishers, New York.

First American Edition

Printed in Great Britain

10 9 8 7 6 5 4 3 2 1

Contents

The armorial bearings of John, 1st
Duke of Marlborough. The
double-headed eagle was the crest
of the Holy Roman Empire of
which he was a prince. The St
George's Cross was granted to the
Duke's father, Sir Winston
Churchill, by Charles II as an
"honourable augmentation".

Foreword

Iam very happy to confirm the statement made in the first chapter of this book that I and my wife have "a genuine affection" for Blenheim. Whatever some of my predecessors may, or may not, have thought about it, we really do love the place and are immensely proud of its great heritage. Mr Montgomery-Massingberd brings the story right up to the present day (even mentioning our newly-opened Butterfly House and Plant Centre) and as he says in the last chapter – aptly entitled "The Present Battle for Blenheim" – we are determined "to keep Blenheim going". We are indeed, not just for future generations of Spencer-Churchills, but for those who wish to visit – and revisit – this supreme example of English baroque architecture set in its magnificent park.

Mr Montgomery-Massingberd's readably condensed and often entertaining version of events, together with the feast of pictures makes this book for me. My favourite vision of Blenheim is in the early evening light of summer and I can honestly say that I have never seen a photograph that captures its magical qualities of warmth and beauty better than Mr Hornak's view on the cover. I have been pleased to give permission for various photographs from the family albums and archives to add to this pictorial celebration.

Marlborough

Blenheim Palace, 1985

SELECT GENEALOGICAL TABLE

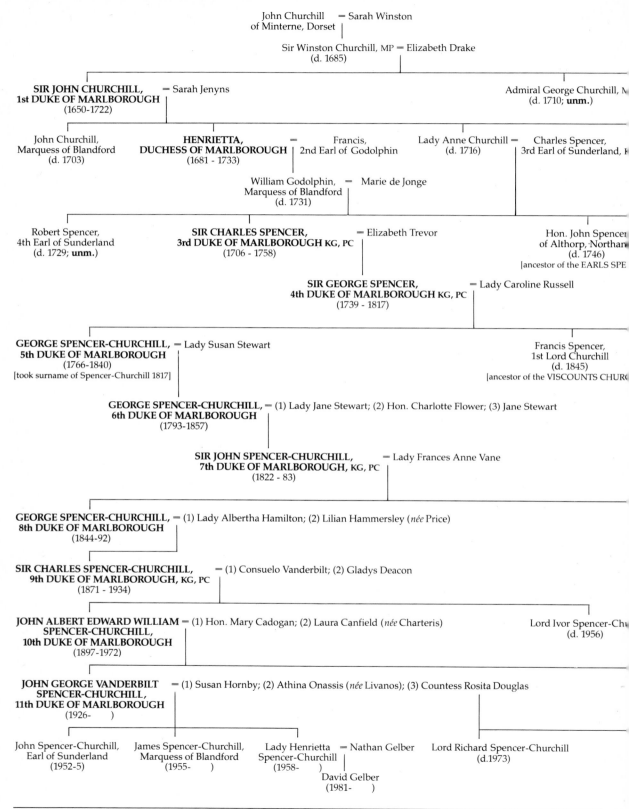

John Churchill of Minterne, Dorset = Sarah Winston

Sir Winston Churchill, MP (d. 1685) = Elizabeth Drake

SIR JOHN CHURCHILL, 1st DUKE OF MARLBOROUGH (1650-1722) = Sarah Jenyns

Admiral George Churchill, N (d. 1710; **unm.**)

John Churchill, Marquess of Blandford (d. 1703)

HENRIETTA, DUCHESS OF MARLBOROUGH (1681 - 1733) = Francis, 2nd Earl of Godolphin

Lady Anne Churchill (d. 1716) = Charles Spencer, 3rd Earl of Sunderland, K

William Godolphin, Marquess of Blandford (d. 1731) = Marie de Jonge

Robert Spencer, 4th Earl of Sunderland (d. 1729; **unm.**)

SIR CHARLES SPENCER, 3rd DUKE OF MARLBOROUGH KG, PC (1706 - 1758) = Elizabeth Trevor

Hon. John Spencer of Althorp, Northam (d. 1746) [ancestor of the EARLS SPE

SIR GEORGE SPENCER, 4th DUKE OF MARLBOROUGH KG, PC (1739 - 1817) = Lady Caroline Russell

GEORGE SPENCER-CHURCHILL, 5th DUKE OF MARLBOROUGH (1766-1840) [took surname of Spencer-Churchill 1817] = Lady Susan Stewart

Francis Spencer, 1st Lord Churchill (d. 1845) [ancestor of the VISCOUNTS CHUR(

GEORGE SPENCER-CHURCHILL, 6th DUKE OF MARLBOROUGH (1793-1857) = (1) Lady Jane Stewart; (2) Hon. Charlotte Flower; (3) Jane Stewart

SIR JOHN SPENCER-CHURCHILL, 7th DUKE OF MARLBOROUGH, KG, PC (1822 - 83) = Lady Frances Anne Vane

GEORGE SPENCER-CHURCHILL, 8th DUKE OF MARLBOROUGH (1844-92) = (1) Lady Albertha Hamilton; (2) Lilian Hammersley (*née* Price)

SIR CHARLES SPENCER-CHURCHILL, 9th DUKE OF MARLBOROUGH, KG, PC (1871 - 1934) = (1) Consuelo Vanderbilt; (2) Gladys Deacon

JOHN ALBERT EDWARD WILLIAM SPENCER-CHURCHILL, 10th DUKE OF MARLBOROUGH (1897-1972) = (1) Hon. Mary Cadogan; (2) Laura Canfield (*née* Charteris)

Lord Ivor Spencer-Chu (d. 1956)

JOHN GEORGE VANDERBILT SPENCER-CHURCHILL, 11th DUKE OF MARLBOROUGH (1926-   ) = (1) Susan Hornby; (2) Athina Onassis (*née* Livanos); (3) Countess Rosita Douglas

John Spencer-Churchill, Earl of Sunderland (1952-5)

James Spencer-Churchill, Marquess of Blandford (1955-   )

Lady Henrietta Spencer-Churchill (1958-   ) = Nathan Gelber

David Gelber (1981-   )

Lord Richard Spencer-Churchill (d.1973)

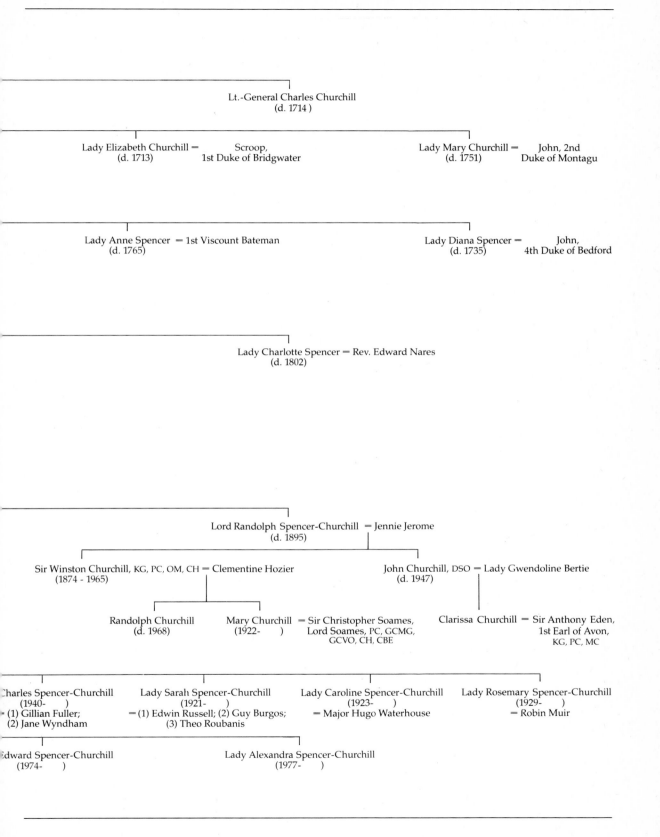

Lt.-General Charles Churchill
(d. 1714)

Lady Elizabeth Churchill =   Scroop,
(d. 1713)   1st Duke of Bridgwater

Lady Mary Churchill =   John, 2nd
(d. 1751)   Duke of Montagu

Lady Anne Spencer = 1st Viscount Bateman
(d. 1765)

Lady Diana Spencer =   John,
(d. 1735)   4th Duke of Bedford

Lady Charlotte Spencer = Rev. Edward Nares
(d. 1802)

Lord Randolph Spencer-Churchill = Jennie Jerome
(d. 1895)

Sir Winston Churchill, KG, PC, OM, CH = Clementine Hozier
(1874 - 1965)

John Churchill, DSO = Lady Gwendoline Bertie
(d. 1947)

Randolph Churchill
(d. 1968)

Mary Churchill = Sir Christopher Soames,
(1922-   )   Lord Soames, PC, GCMG,
GCVO, CH, CBE

Clarissa Churchill = Sir Anthony Eden,
1st Earl of Avon,
KG, PC, MC

Charles Spencer-Churchill
(1940-   )
= (1) Gillian Fuller;
(2) Jane Wyndham

Lady Sarah Spencer-Churchill
(1921-   )
= (1) Edwin Russell; (2) Guy Burgos;
(3) Theo Roubanis

Lady Caroline Spencer-Churchill
(1923-   )
= Major Hugo Waterhouse

Lady Rosemary Spencer-Churchill
(1929-   )
= Robin Muir

Edward Spencer-Churchill
(1974-   )

Lady Alexandra Spencer-Churchill
(1977-   )

1. "Nothing to equal this"

"**G**reat barrack of a place," reports Hooper to Captain Charles Ryder at the beginning of Evelyn Waugh's novel *Brideshead Revisited*. "I've just had a snoop round. Very ornate I'd call it." Today some half-a-million Hoopers a year enter Capability Brown's ravishing park for a snoop round Vanbrugh's ornately baroque palace, built in honour of the 1st Duke of Marlborough's great victory at Blindheim, or Blenheim, in Bavaria on 13 August 1704. Ever since building operations began on the old royal estate of Woodstock, granted by "a munificent sovereign", Queen Anne, to the triumphant Marlborough in 1705, Blenheim has always received somewhat mixed notices from its visitors.

"That celebrated palace," noted Arthur Young in *A Southern Tour* (1767), "which has been by some so excessively abused, and so praised by others. The front is a clutter of parts, so distinct that a Gothic Church has as much unity; and withal, a heaviness in each part, which is infinitely disgusting." That inveterate sight-seer considered the palace to consist "of such innumerable and trifling parts, that one would think them the fragments of a rock jumbled together by an earthquake." It is possible that both Young's intemperate views and those of another celebrated eighteenth-century onlooker, Horace Walpole, may have been influenced by the disobliging behaviour of the palace staff. Young recorded "the excessive insolence of the porters at the park-gate, and at that into the courtyard"; he witnessed "their abusing a single gentleman in a very scurrilous manner, for not feeing them after giving the house-porter half a crown for seeing it". Walpole, who summed up Blenheim as "execrable within, without, & almost all round", found the palace inhabited only by "a cross housekeeper and an impertinent porter" in the 1730s, when it was suffering from one of its periodic bouts of neglect. Again, in the nineteenth century, Prince Puckler-Muskau was not impressed by "some very dirty shabby servants" who produced an imperious housekeeper, wrapped in Scotch plaid, to show him "many chill and faded rooms".

That there is nothing new in the visitor business is illustrated by the 5th Viscount Torrington's description in his diary for August 1787 of "following a great crowd" into the palace and then falling in "with a corps of 30 observers – what a plague and fatigue". Apart from finding the works of Rubens (later sold by the 8th Duke) "disgusting and indecent", Lord Torrington was

Opposite: Queen Anne presents an elevation of Blenheim to "Military Merit". An allegorical painting by Kneller.

moved, on a later visit, to protest in his diary about the 4th Duke of Marlborough's harsh treatment of the birds at Blenheim: "Oh fye! – What for a few cherries, destroy all the songsters?... 'Stretch forth, Marlborough, thy hand of mercy, and of pity; and let not infamous slaughter prevail.'" Mrs Arbuthnot was shocked to record of her visit to Blenheim in 1824, in company with the Duke of Wellington, that "People may shoot and fish at so much per hour!" A century later, on the credit side, Lytton Strachey was enthusing: "There is a bridge over a lake which positively gives one an erection."

Laura, Duchess of Marlborough, the widow of Bert, the 10th Duke, has described Blenheim as "so terribly gloomy". It was, she wrote in her racy memoirs, "built as a monument, not a house to live in", and she always referred to the palace as "the Dump". Sir Winston Churchill, Blenheim's most famous son, and heir to the dukedom of Marlborough until Bert's birth in 1897, maintained loyally that "the cumulative labours of Vanbrugh and 'Capability' Brown have succeeded at Blenheim in setting an Italian palace in an English park without apparent incongruity", but many visitors have echoed Laura's point of view. However much they might admire the dramatic splendour of Vanbrugh's triumphal creation, few visitors would want to live within the stately walls. It is noticeable that Blenheim seems to crop up most often in a negative sense, in such remarks as "so-and-so has a special atmosphere, not like Blenheim", or "you don't want to live in a Blenheim-style palace".

To complain of the palace's lack of homeliness, however, is rather beside the point. The object, after all, was not only to house a national hero, but to celebrate England's newly-won supremacy over the French in a blaze of architectural glory that rivalled Versailles. The triumphal mood of Vanbrugh's dramatic composition is everywhere apparent – from the Gibbons carvings of English lions lacerating French cocks on the towers to the trophies on the entrance steps underneath the portico presided over by Pallas Minerva, goddess of victory. On the ceiling of the cool marbled Great Hall within, Marlborough, attired by Sir James Thornhill as a Roman General, shows the Blenheim battle plan to Britannia. The ceiling of the Saloon, painted by Louis Laguerre, shows the victorious Duke driving a chariot through the sky. The Duke's armorial bearings, complete with the black double-headed eagle – the crest of the Holy Roman Empire of which he was a prince – are displayed over the doors. In the Green Writing-Room hangs the tapestry of Marlborough accepting Marshal Tallard's surrender at the Battle of Blenheim; more tapestries of his great victories adorn the three State Rooms. The State apartments at Blenheim were, naturally, intended not to be "lived in" (the family have always been based in the east wing) but as courtly chambers in which to entertain the sovereign. Queen Anne, an unlikely figure to preside over an age of national glory, is commemorated in the Library by a Rysbrack statue commissioned after the Duke's death by the Queen's erstwhile friend, Duchess Sarah. In the Chapel, Marlborough, dressed in Roman armour, stands atop a monument so noble as to make the visitor wonder whether one is supposed to be worshipping God or the Great Duke. In the park, the Duke, again dressed as a Roman General, surmounts the Column of Victory.

The Churchills, like Blenheim itself, have also long aroused differing emotions. Swift said of the 1st Duke that he was "as covetous as Hell"; Chesterton compared him to Judas Iscariot. A clue to the fiery Duchess Sarah's character can be obtained from the fact that she embarked upon 400 lawsuits. The 4th Duke of Marlborough, who did so much for Blenheim as the patron of Capability Brown and William Chambers, was, according to the gossip of *The Jockey Club* (1792), "sullen and overbearing in his general demeanour". The 6th Duke was involved in a court case "gravely reflecting on his moral character"; and then there was the "wicked" 8th Duke, who sold so many of Blenheim's treasures in the 1880s, and his erratic brother Lord Randolph Churchill (Winston's father). The 9th Duke, though one of the most important figures in the Blenheim story on account of his re-formalizing the gardens and other major works, was a strange and unhappy man whose marital career amply illustrates how singularly inappropriate was his sobriquet of "Sunny". Viscountess Churchill, the wife of another peer descended from the denizens of Blenheim, when commiserating with the 9th Duke's second wife, Gladys Deacon, spoke of "all the ungentle-manlike tricks that the family we both had the misfortune to marry into can do – the lies and spite". The 10th Duke, possibly one of the least appreciated comic figures in the twentieth-century aristocracy, became a byword for antediluvian attitudes. Various voices have complained of the Churchills' vulgarity, philistinism and arrogance, talking of "bad blood" somewhere along the line. And yet the pedigree has produced two national heroes in the 1st Duke and Sir Winston Churchill.

Is Blenheim, then, an unpleasant place lived in by unpleasant people, or rather the proudest part of the heritage, the seat of our most distinguished dynasty? Few would deny that Blenheim is the greatest palace in Britain (in James Lees-Milne's view the Saloon "can vie with the most splendid palace rooms in Europe"), far outstripping those in the possession of the royal family; George III sagely remarked that he had "nothing to equal this". The particular charm and beauty of the honey-coloured palace is often an acquired taste; Blenheim needs to be revisited. Much depends on the love it receives from its owners; in the present generation Blenheim is fortunate in having a Duke and Duchess of Marlborough who have a genuine affection for the place. Blenheim's vicissitudes and those of the frequently mis-understood Spencer-Churchills are intertwined.

Above: One of Grinling Gibbons's stone carvings, showing an English lion lacerating a French cock, that triumphantly adorn Vanbrugh's towers.

Left: The Marlborough monument by Rysbrack in Blenheim Chapel, showing the victorious Duke dressed as a Roman General.

Opposite: The ceiling in the Great Hall painted by Sir James Thornhill in 1716. Marlborough kneels in front of Britannia and shows her a plan of the Battle of Blenheim.

John Duke of Marlborough

2. "That once was a man"

Born plain John Churchill near Axminster in Devon in the middle of the seventeenth century, the national hero for whom Blenheim Palace was built ended up as Duke of Marlborough, Marquess of Blandford, Earl of Marlborough, Lord Churchill of Eyemouth, Lord Churchill of Sandridge – and a Prince of the Holy Roman Empire and Prince of Mindelheim in Swabia for good measure. He remains one of the very few men in British history (other European countries furnish plenty of examples) to have risen from obscure beginnings to a dukedom. Indeed, the dukedom of Marlborough is the only one now in existence to have been conferred on a man who was born the son of a commoner with no prospect of inheriting either a title or large estates. For though the great Duke of Wellington, with whom Marlborough is unendingly compared, might likewise be thought of as a "self-made duke", he was in fact the younger son of an earl – and his own son eventually succeeded to the family earldom as well as the dukedom. The large majority of British ducal families have moved gradually up the scale of the peerage. John Churchill rocketed to his dukedom, collecting two baronies, an earldom and a marquessate on the way.

The beginnings were not, however, as obscure as all that; those of successful "achievers" in Britain seldom are. The Churchills were a long-established West Country family of minor gentry possessing that badge of nobility, a coat of arms. Discounting their fanciful claim to be descended from Roger de Courcil, alleged companion-in-arms to William the Conqueror, it seems that a descent from Charles Churchill who married Margaret Woodville (or Widville), kinswoman of Edward IV's Queen, can be accepted. Originally from Devon, the Churchills later moved to Dorset and, in the usual way, improved their standing through judicious marriages. In 1618 the great commander's grandfather and namesake, John Churchill of Minterne near Dorchester, and of the Middle Temple in London, married Sarah Winston, the heiress of a Gloucestershire landowner. Their son, named Winston in his mother's honour, did even better in marrying Elizabeth Drake, daughter of Sir John Drake, the squire of Ashe in Devon. The Drakes were a distinguished Devonian dynasty – to which Sir Francis, the celebrated Elizabethan sea-dog, had claimed to belong – and Sir John's wife was also niece of James I's powerful favourite George Villiers, Duke of Buckingham (another and much less worthy example of a

Opposite: "That once was a man." John, 1st Duke of Marlborough painted by Sir Godfrey Kneller.

Left: John and Sarah Churchill with their young family in 1693. Painting by Closterman.

Above: Arabella Churchill, sister of the 1st Duke of Marlborough and mistress of James II.

ducal ascent from modest origins). Elizabeth Churchill's maternal aunts were the Countesses of Chichester, Marlborough (a title then held by the Ley family) and Newport; Lady Howard of Escrick; and Mrs Endymion Porter, the wife of Buckingham's toady. Clearly the Churchills had arrived.

Unfortunately the family fortunes, considerably enhanced by the Drake marriage, swiftly collapsed as a result of the Civil War which ruined so many loyal Cavaliers. Educated at Oxford, Winston Churchill was an ardent royalist, serving Charles I as a Captain of Horse and impoverishing himself in the King's cause. Charles II later awarded Winston an honourable augmentation of a St George's Cross to the Churchill coat of arms for service to his father, and also a knighthood, but no pecuniary compensations.

There are striking parallels between the careers of the first Sir Winston Churchill and his more celebrated namesake and descendant. Both were soldiers, and cavalrymen at that; both were politicians (the first Sir Winston represented Weymouth in the Restoration Parliament and later Lyme Regis); both were staunch "King's men"; both were authors (the first Sir Winston published *Divi Britannici* in 1675); and both were inclined to be short of, not to say confused by, cash. The honours heaped on the first Sir Winston by Charles II, well deserved though they were, did nothing to improve the Churchillian coffers. He had been fined £4,446 (a colossal sum in those days) by the victorious Parliament and had suffered the ignominious fate of having to retreat under his Puritanical Cromwellian mother-in-law's roof (which had, to pile cruel irony on insult and injury, been knocked about by the royalists). The Stuarts being perennially hard-up themselves (one of the causes of the Civil War in the first place), nothing was done at the Restoration to compensate ruined Cavaliers like Sir Winston, so he found himself obliged to seek employment. He became Commissioner of the Court of Claims in Ireland and then Junior Clerk Comptroller of the King's Household in Whitehall, but money continued to be an almost crippling worry until his death in 1688. This background of grinding, genteel poverty obviously left its mark on the great Marlborough, making him so extraordinarily careful – his arch-critics, such as Macaulay, would insist on "mean and grasping" – with money.

The second Sir Winston Churchill wrote in his passionately anti-Macaulay biography of the 1st Duke of Marlborough that "we know as much of the early years of Alexander the Great, Hannibal and Julius Caesar [one need hardly add that these names were not chosen at random] as we do of this figure separated from us by scarcely a couple of centuries." John was the third son of Sir Winston and Lady Churchill (of the others, six in all, George, a bachelor, became an Admiral and a politician; and Charles, married but childless, a Lieutenant-General and

Governor of Brussels after the Battle of Blenheim). John was born at his maternal grandmother's battered home of Ashe on 24 June 1650, where the atmosphere is likely to have been less than harmonious.

Young Jack received brief spells of education at the Corporation City School in Dublin while his father was working in Ireland, and at St Paul's School in London (later, incidentally, the *alma mater* of the Second World War commander, Viscount Montgomery of Alamein who liked to compare himself to his fellow "M"). Then, at the age of fifteen, he became a page to James, Duke of York, Charles II's unpopular, if equally lusty, brother. Jack's elder sister, Arabella, was already employed as a maid of honour to the Duchess of York (the former Anne Hyde) in the same household – where, as in other parts of the court, the children of loyal Cavaliers were welcome recruits. Arabella duly went on to share the Duke's bed, bearing him several bastards (including James FitzJames, Duke of Berwick, who became a Marshal of France and fought against his uncle Jack). Thus Arabella Churchill can be counted as one of the seventeenth-century royal mistresses who helped to found English ducal houses – Charles II's liaisons with Barbara Villiers, Louise de Kéroualle, Nell Gwynn and Lucy Walters accounting for the others – for there is no question that the great Duke of Marlborough owed his early advancement to the fact that his sister was the Duke of York's doxy.

"The Duke of York's love for his sister first brought him to Court," noted the nosy John Macky, "and the beauty of his own person and his good address so gained on the Duchess of Cleveland that she effectually established him there." The Duchess, better known as Charles II's tempestuous mistress, Barbara Villiers (ancestress of the Dukes of Grafton) was herself a kinswoman of Jack's, but her interest in the young man was not, as Macky intimates, merely cousinly. The diarist John Evelyn and other contemporary observers noted the youthful Churchill's tall, handsome, noble and graceful appearance. Lord Chesterfield thought "his figure was beautiful but his manner was irresistible", while Bishop Burnet was impressed by "his clever head and sound judgement". The inevitable affair between the rapacious older woman (Barbara was nine years Jack's senior) and the ambitious young courtier seems to have begun in 1671; a bastard daughter was born the following year. Two stories, both of questionable veracity, are often told of their relationship. In one, Charles II encounters Churchill in *flagrante delicto* with Barbara and says to him: "Go to! You are a rascal, but I forgive you because you do it to get your bread." In the other version, Jack jumps out of her window in the nick of time before the King makes his theatrically signalled entrance, and Barbara later rewards her athletic swain with a lavish tip of £5,000. This would account for how he was able, at the age of twenty-four, to buy an

Sarah, Duchess of Marlborough playing cards with Lady Fitzharding. Painting by Kneller.

Elizabeth, Countess of Bridgwater, the Duke's third daughter, who died in 1713.

Above: The famous Blenheim despatch, scribbled by Marlborough on the back of a tavern bill, asking his wife to tell the Queen that "her army has had a glorious victory".

Right: The quit-rent standard presented to the sovereign every year on the anniversary of the Battle of Blenheim as "rent" for the palace.

annuity of £500 from Lord Halifax for £4,500. Whether Barbara got good value from her young stud is another matter; she is said to have remarked that he had cost her a good deal of money "for very little service".

With so little known for sure of Marlborough's early life, it is inevitable that legends loom large. Another – inviting enough, like all such stories – goes that when he was watching the Guards in Hyde Park with his royal master, the Duke of York, the boy page pleaded for "a pair of colours in one of those fine regiments". And so, on 24 September 1667, John Churchill was commissioned an ensign in the King's Regiment of Foot Guards. The military career of the greatest soldier in the history of the British army was under way.

His baptism of fire, though, had a strongly nautical flavour. He was on board ship for the blockade of Algiers in 1670 (his first posting was three years fighting the Moors in North Africa) and for the battles with the Dutch around the English coast in 1672. Following the Battle of Sole Bay off Southwold in June 1672, he was promoted to Captain in the Lord High Admiral's Regiment (the Lord High Admiral being his patron, the Duke of York). In October, however, Sir Winston was complaining that his "poor son Jack" had been "very unfortunate ever since in the continuance of the King's displeasure [over Barbara Villiers, presumably] . . . notwithstanding the service he did in the last fight", and that Jack had been confined to his "country quarters at Yarmouth". But Captain Churchill did not languish out of favour for long and in 1673 went off to France (then England's ally against the Dutch) to serve in the Royal English Regiment of the French army, under the command of Charles II's bastard son, the Duke of Monmouth. He was wounded at the Siege of Maastricht, thanked by Louis XIV, *Le Roi Soleil* in person, promoted to be a Colonel in the French army, and gained useful experience in Alsace and southern Germany under the brilliant French commander Henri, Vicomte du Turenne.

In 1676 Churchill was offered the command of the Royal English Regiment, but turned it down for reasons which the French shrewdly attributed to romance. The object of his affections was another member of the Yorks' entourage, Sarah Jenyns ("Jennings" is an anachronism), who came from a similar, slightly reduced, squirearchical background. The youngest daughter of the late Richard Jenyns, of Sandridge, Hertfordshire – strangely enough sometime Lord of the Manor of Churchill in Somerset, an estate bought by his family in 1563 – and sister of Frances, "La Belle Jenyns", the Duchess of Tyrconnell, Sarah became a maid of honour aged only thirteen to the new Duchess of York (Mary of Modena) in 1673. As Pepys observed, "there was nothing almost but bawdry at court from top to bottom" in Restoration times and ladies-in-waiting were regarded as easy game. The anxious Mrs Jenyns tried to remove Sarah in 1676 because "two of the maids of honour had had great bellies at court and she would not leave her child there to have the third", but the already formidably determined girl preserved her position and her virginity. By this time she was already conducting a spirited courtship with John Churchill (free of La Cleveland's clutches and utterly hooked by the beautiful teenager) that has been aptly compared by Peter Quennell to that between Congreve's Mirabell and Millamant in *The Way of the World*.

"If it were true," wrote the sixteen-year-old Sarah, resisting the army Adonis's advances, "that you have the passion for me which you say you have, you would find out some way to make yourself happy – it is in your power. Therefore press me no more to see you, since it is what I cannot in honour approve of and, if I have done too much, be so just as to consider who was the cause of it."

To which her suitor replied, on the attack: "You say I pretend a passion for you when I have other things in my head. I cannot imagine what you mean by it, for I vow to God that you do so entirely possess my thoughts that I think of nothing else in this world but your own dear self."

Later in their lives, during the household squabbles of Queen Anne's reign, the Duke of Marlborough remarked to Sarah: "I do very much agree with you that happiness is seldom found in a court." None the less, an outstanding exception to this rule was their own romance which burgeoned in the Yorks' court and blossomed into one of the happiest recorded marriages in British history.

"Wherever you are whilst I have life," Sarah wrote to her husband sometime after he had received the earldom of Marlborough in 1689, "my soul shall follow you, my ever dear Lord Marlborough; and wherever I am I should only kill the time, wish for night that I may sleep and hope the next day to hear from you." After his death she refused the "Proud" Duke of Somerset's offer of marriage with spirited loyalty: "If I were young and handsome as I was, instead of old and faded as I am, and you could lay the empire of the world at my feet, you should never share the heart and head that once belonged to John, Duke of Marlborough."

The exact date of their marriage has never been conclusively established, although it probably took place during the winter of 1677-8 in the apartments of the Duchess of York, who is traditionally supposed to have been present. The Duke of York found Jack Churchill, promoted to an English colonelcy in 1676, a capable agent for various missions at home and abroad, particularly when the tactless heir to the throne, who never disguised his conversion to Catholicism, was obliged to go into exile to Holland and Scotland in the wake of Titus Oates's allegations of a "Popish Plot" that washed over London like a wave of filth. Churchill was thus able to gain useful experience in the arts of

Overleaf: The surrender of Marshal Tallard depicted on the famous Blenheim Tapestry, commissioned by the 1st Duke to commemorate his great victory. It now hangs in the Green Writing-Room.

HOOGHSTET

diplomacy, not to say intrigue, laying the foundations of his eventual career as a statesman, while his military talents lay fallow in a period of peace. As the Duke of York's envoy Churchill encountered his master's distinctly Protestant son-in-law, William of Orange, a shrewd manipulator of the European chessboard. It was an acquaintance that was to prove highly significant.

For the moment, however, Churchill's star was still hitched to the Duke of York's wagon. This began to roll again in 1681 when the Yorks returned to London after Charles II had ridden out Parliament's attempts to exclude his brother from the throne. The following year Churchill entered the peerage of Scotland as Lord Churchill of Eyemouth and in 1683 he was appointed Colonel of the Royal Regiment of Dragoons. As a key member of the Yorks' household, he went over to collect their daughter Princess Anne's uninspiring future husband, Prince George of Denmark, and bring him back to England for the nuptials. Anne had formed an attachment to Jack's wife, Sarah, five years her senior, during the family's exile, and so the new Lady Churchill of Eyemouth became the married Princess's Lady of the Bed-chamber. Soon any traces of formality at the Cockpit, Anne's residence in Whitehall, between the rather gauche Princess and the domineering Sarah disappeared; the two friends would cosily address, and refer to, each other as "Mrs Morley" and "Mrs Freeman" respectively.

Upon the accession of his patron, the Duke of York, to the throne as James II in 1685, Churchill's star was in the ascendant. He ranked second among the new King's Gentlemen of the Bedchamber, served briefly as Ambassador to Louis XIV in Paris, became a Governor of the Hudson's Bay Company and received a barony in the English peerage (as Lord Churchill of Sandridge). He was also promoted Major-General in the army and Colonel of the 3rd Troop of Horse Guards after he had won his spurs in the same year when he was to the fore in smashing the 'Pitchfork Rebellion' in the West Country led by James II's nephew, the Duke of Monmouth, at the Battle of Sedgemoor. As the military historian Correlli Barnett has pointed out, Sedgemoor 'displayed Churchill at a turning-point in his development as a soldier . . . the able regimental officer was maturing into a General of quick and complete strategic grasp, well able to bear the moral weight of independent command in the field.''

James II himself soon proved rather less suited to monarchy. Devoid of tact, he proceeded to embark on the disastrous policy of appointing Catholics to key positions. As fears of Popery grew apace, in the confines of the Cockpit, the Churchills and Princess Anne secretly determined to stick to their Protestantism what-ever the consequences. The Princess told her sister Mary, the wife of William of Orange, that she was "resolved to undergo anything rather than change my religion"; and Churchill wrote to his old acquaintance William that "my places and the King's favour I set at nought, in comparison of being true to my religion." In judging Churchill's behaviour towards his benefactor, James II, the contemporary religious climate has always to be borne in mind. The Civil War, only a generation previously, had, after all, been fought merely between the forces of High Anglicanism and Puritanism. With the birth of a son and heir to the King and Queen in June 1688, unfortunately coinciding with the nadir of James's popularity, the prospect of a Catholic dynasty became intolerable.

That November William of Orange, the Prince regarded as the Protestant saviour, landed in Devon, with the Dutch army in tow, and advanced on Salisbury where James II had pitched camp. Although he had been secretly instrumental in encouraging the invasion, Lieutenant-General (as he now was) Lord Churchill had ridden west with the royal army. "Churchill," wrote G.K. Chesterton in his book, *A Short History of England*, "as if to add something ideal to his imitation of Iscariot, went to James with wanton professions of love and loyalty, went forth in arms as if to defend the country from the invasion, and then calmly handed over the country to the invader." But while Churchill's conduct was undeniably underhand, it must be remembered that he was not alone in this; as James II himself remarked, "God help me! My very children have forsaken me." Princess Anne was spirited away by Sarah down the back stairs of the Cockpit and off to Nottinghamshire. Her husband, George of Denmark, joined Churchill in the camp of the wretched King's other son-in-law, William of Orange, the beneficiary of the "Bloodless Revolution".

A couple of days before the Coronation of the Prince and Princess of Orange as King William III and Queen Mary II in April 1689, Lord Churchill of Sandridge was advanced in the English peerage to become Earl of Marlborough. The new Earl had no property in this Wiltshire town or in its vicinity, but probably chose the title because it had previously been held by his maternal great-uncle, James Ley, and was now extinct. In addition to the earldom, he became a Privy Councillor and was confirmed as a Lieutenant-General in the army (with responsibility for its reconstruction) and also as a Gentleman of the Bedchamber. But the hopes he must have had of a position of greatly increased power after the key role he had played in the overthrow of James II were dashed by the new King's importation of his own favourites from Holland. Instead, the new Lord Marlborough could only shine in a comparatively subdued light as an able, not to say over-zealous, army administrator or as the commander of the forces that conducted successful forays against the French at the Battle of Walcourt in Flanders and against their Irish allies at Kinsale and Cork. He made no secret of his disgruntlement with "Dutch William", which was matched

Left: In the Bouchain Tapestry in the Second State Room, the dog appears to have been given horse's hooves.

In the same room hangs a portrait of Louis XIV who forbade any mention of the Battle of Blenheim in his presence. Painting by Mignard.

Anne, Countess of Sunderland, Marlborough's second daughter. Her son became the 3rd Duke of Marlborough and the title has passed in direct line of descent ever since.

by Sarah's disenchantment with Queen Mary, who tried to prevent Lady Marlborough's royal mistress, Princess Anne, from receiving an independent income from Parliament. In January 1692, after the Marlboroughs had used their influence to secure the Princess her "Civil List" money, the enraged Queen Mary instructed her sister to sack Sarah from her household. Princess Anne declined, but the following morning King William dismissed Lord Marlborough from all his posts, accusing him of intriguing with the exiled James II in France.

The suspicion appears to have been well grounded. In the light of Marlborough's extraordinary turn and turnabout, even the late Sir Winston Churchill's defence of his ancestor ("Those who write with crude censure of the shame of deserting James for William or William for James seem to forget that James or William were not ends in themselves . . . unswerving fidelity to a particular king was no test of . . . virtue or baseness.") seems somewhat special pleading. May 1692 found Marlborough languishing in the Tower of London on a charge of High Treason, although he was released after six weeks when it was proved that he had been the victim of a Jacobite plot ("framed" by a forged letter). Another cause of his falling foul of King William had been his already notorious "venality". According to the diarist John Evelyn, Lord Marlborough was dismissed "for his excessive taking of bribes, covetousness, and extortion on all occasions, from his inferior officers". In fairness it must be said that Marlborough always showed concern for the welfare of the men under his command, but this reputation for meanness – the story went that neither Jack nor Sarah dotted their "i's" in order to save ink – was to dog the Marlboroughs and was ultimately to provide the excuse for their undoing.

Following Marlborough's release from the Tower, the future looked distinctly unpromising. However, the heir to the throne, Princess Anne, remained a staunch ally and after the death of the Princess's sister, Queen Mary, in 1694, the Marlboroughs' position improved. Thanks to the Princess's good offices, Marlborough was given the fairly undemanding task of being Governor to her young son, the Duke of Gloucester (the only child of the unfortunate Anne to survive infancy, though even he only lived until he was eleven), the second in line to the throne. By the end of the century Marlborough had been restored to favour as a Privy Councillor, Cabinet Minister, a Lord Justice or "Regent" (during the King's absences abroad) and Master of the Horse. The threat to the balance of power in Europe posed by the question of the Spanish Succession removed any further doubts William III may have had about giving Marlborough the command which his military talents had long deserved. As Dutch William grudgingly admitted in 1690: "No officer living who has seen so little service as my Lord Marlborough, is so fit for great commands."

Before Charles II, the last King of the Spanish Habsburg line, died in 1700, and his will was known, Louis XIV of France and the other Great Powers of Europe agreed to carve up the Spanish dominions after Charles's death. The old Habsburg then set the cat among the pigeons by naming Louis XIV's grandson, Philip of Anjou, as his heir in the will. Louis XIV decided to go back on his partition treaties with England and the United Provinces and allowed his grandson to become King of the whole Spanish empire. The French monarch aggravated the situation from the English point of view by recognizing James II's son as "James III" in the face of the Act of Settlement of 1701, which specifically excluded the male line of the Stuarts from the English throne and settled the crown on the Protestant Hanoverian line.

Louis's actions provoked a full-scale European war – the War of the Spanish Succession or, as they came to be known in honour of the great soldier's epic series of victories, "Marlborough's Wars". In 1701 William III formed a Grand Alliance between England, Holland, the Holy Roman Empire, Hanover and Prussia against the combined forces of France, Spain, Bavaria and Savoy. Marlborough was made Commander-in-Chief of the British and Dutch forces in the Netherlands and when William III died in the New Year, following a fall from his horse which had stumbled on a molehill in the park of Hampton Court, he became, as the late King had willed, the new military leader of the Grand Alliance.

At the age of fifty-two – rather late in the day for a soldier, though his still handsome figure belied his years – Marlborough now found himself positioned on an extraordinarily powerful platform for the son of an impoverished West Country squire. Abroad, if he could manage to vanquish the French as General-issimo of the Allied forces, Europe would be at his feet. At home, the accession of his wife's devoted friend Queen Anne ensured that the Marlboroughs' own political-military alliance was well secured. He was immediately nominated for the highest Order of Chivalry, the Garter, which he had long coveted.

War was declared in May 1702 and in the autumn Marlborough enjoyed some early success in the Netherlands campaign against the French, taking Venloo, Stevenswaert, Rüremonde and finally Liège. As a reward, he received from Queen Anne, still firmly under Sarah's thumb, the honours he had hoped for from William III – a marquessate and a dukedom, plus a grant of £5,000 a year during the Queen's life. On 14 December 1702 he became Marquess of Blandford and Duke of Marlborough.

Sadly, though, the heir to the dukedom, the Marlboroughs' only surviving son, John ("Jack"), lived only a few weeks to enjoy his courtesy title of Lord Blandford, dying of smallpox at Cambridge in February 1703. The new Duke, an emotional man, was devastated by grief. Sarah became almost unhinged, taking out her anguish in baseless accusations of infidelity against her somewhat preoccupied husband. A few years later an Act of Parliament enabled the dukedom to pass to his daughters, and thence to their male heirs, in order of seniority – Henrietta or Harriet (who married the 2nd Earl of Godolphin, son of Sidney Godolphin, Queen Anne's chief minister and the Marlboroughs' crony from Cockpit days); Anne (who married the Earl of Sunderland); Elizabeth (who married the Duke of Bridgwater); and Mary (who married the Earl (later Duke) of Montagu).

After this encouraging start to the new Duke's campaign, the situation stagnated. While the Allied armies were marking time up in the Spanish Netherlands in 1703, the French and the Bavarians were threatening to strike at the heart of the Holy Roman Empire. Marlborough saw that the only way to save the situation was to march his troops south into Germany and cut the French off before they reached Vienna. It was a sensationally daring scheme. As he told Sidney Godolphin, "I am very sensible that I take a great deal upon me. But should I act otherwise, the Empire would be undone, and consequently the confederacy."

Like most good ideas, the strategy of the great march south was straightforward enough (the Danube or bust), but its execution was quite another matter. The logistics Marlborough and his Quartermaster-General, William Cadogan, had to cope with were phenomenally complex – 250 miles over and down rivers with 40,000 men (rising to some 56,000 before the end), 19,000 horses, 1,700 wagons, 4,000 draught beasts and the travelling beef rations. In May 1704 Marlborough and his army set off to join forces with the Imperial commander, Prince Eugène of Savoy, whom he met at Mundelsheim in early June.

The Prince found the Duke "a man of high intelligence, of gallantry, well-disposed, and determined to achieve something, all the more so because he would be discredited in England if he returned there, having accomplished nothing. With all these qualities he knows well enough that one does not become a General overnight, and is unassuming about himself." The great European General was apparently equally impressed by "the lively air which I see in every one of those troopers' faces". The two commanders were soon joined by the Margrave of Baden, with whom Marlborough mounted an attack on the Elector of Bavaria at the Schellenberg on 2 July 1704, while Prince Eugène headed off the French Marshals on the Rhine.

The Schellenberg was the first time Marlborough had been in the thick of a real battle since the Siege of Kinsale fourteen years previously. It was a ferocious affair, with the Allies losing some 1,500 men and only a fifth of the 15,000-strong garrison escaping. The Schellenberg Tapestry – one of the marvellously detailed, accurate and almost contemporary series Marlborough himself commissioned from de Hondt, the designer, and Judocus de Vos, the Brussels weaver, to record his triumphant campaigns – hangs in the First State Room, off the Saloon, in Blenheim Palace. It shows the Duke preparing to storm the hilltop fortress. In the foreground of the tapestry, dragoons are loading up their mounts with faggots to be used by the foot-soldiers crossing the Bavarian trenches; in the background the walled city of Donauwörth prepares to defend itself.

A few anxious weeks later, in August 1704, both armies were jockeying on either side of the Danube for the best battle positions. The inevitable conflict would clearly be decisive for the future of Vienna and the Empire. Marshal Tallard and the Franco-Bavarian army of some 60,000 men made camp on the north bank of the river between two obscure villages called Lutzingen and Blindheim, or Blenheim.

It was an alarmingly strong position. Blenheim itself, on the right wing, was a fortress-like affair made up of stone farm-houses; the Nebel, a tributary of the Danube, protected the French front between Blenheim and the village of Oberglau, situated on a slight eminence in the left-centre; while on the left flank stood Lutzingen, surrounded by difficult terrain. Marl-borough drew up his army opposite the French centre in the early morning of 13 August while the engineers set to work building bridges across the Nebel. The French were rudely awakened by Marlborough's manoeuvres ("I rubbed my eyes in disbelief," recalled one of the French Generals afterwards) and fired the first shot near Blenheim at about eight o'clock. Tallard swiftly decided to set a trap for Marlborough by tempting him over the Nebel in the centre so that the two French wings could close in on the Allies from both sides. To defend the vulnerable right wing the French packed Blenheim with infantry battalions.

Marlborough was obliged to delay the full-scale action until he heard word that Prince Eugène was in a position to lead the attack on the French left flank. The message eventually reached him at about half past twelve. Then Lord Cutts was ordered to begin the assault on Blenheim and Marlborough's brother, General Charles Churchill, to advance on the Nebel in the centre. Cutts's infantry, under Brigadier Rowe, soon ran into trouble and looked like being annihilated by the French cavalry; but Marlborough despatched supporting cavalry under General Palmes to the rescue. This resulted in an uplifting rout of the French Gendarmerie (a prestigious cavalry regiment, inci-dentally, not mounted policemen). As Cutts's men reached the village of Blenheim, the French commander of the right wing, Clérambault, panicked, piling yet more infantry battalions into the garrison. The French centre was thus weakened and Marl-borough was able to form up his crucial array in the middle ground pretty much as he pleased.

But the battle was not over yet. The Allied attack on the French left-centre stronghold of Oberglau under Prince Holstein-Beck, which came at about three in the afternoon, was a near-disaster.

The French counter-attack had to be checked by the quick-thinking Marlborough himself until reinforcements switched from Prince Eugène's troops engaged on the French left wing were able to save the day. The long hot afternoon wore bloodily on. By five o'clock Marlborough was able to give the order for the final cavalry charge against the beleaguered enemy. The French, who had fondly imagined they were invincible, turned tail and fled ignominiously, many of them straight into the Danube. It was indeed a smashing, famous victory – one which *Le Roi Soleil*, whose forces were virtually cut in half, banned from ever being mentioned in his presence.

"I have not time to say more," scribbled the triumphant Duke of Marlborough on the only scrap of paper to hand, "but to beg you will give my duty to the Queen, and let her know her army has had a glorious victory. Monsieur Tallard and two other Generals are in my coach, and I am following the rest. The bearer, my aide-de-camp, Colonel Parkes, will give her an account of what has passed. I shall do it in a day or two by another more at large." This dispatch, written to Sarah on the back of a tavern bill for food and drink, is still preserved in the First State Room at Blenheim Palace.

In the same room is kept the Blenheim Standard, decorated with the three French fleurs-de-lis, one of which is sent every year to the sovereign at Windsor Castle on the anniversary of the great battle (13 August) as "quit-rent" for the royal Manor of Woodstock in Oxfordshire, the site of the future "Blenheim Palace", which was granted to the Duke of Marlborough as a reward in January 1705.

The most important of all the tapestries in the palace, the Blenheim Tapestry, showing Marlborough accepting Marshal Tallard's surrender, hangs in the Green Writing-Room. Close scrutiny of the faithfully-reproduced scene is tantamount to being an eye-witness of the battle, so colourful and exact is this superb example of the weaver's art. Behind the Grenadier can be seen a field dressing-station, watermills ablaze, the village of Blenheim full of French troops and, in the distance, the Allies pursuing the enemy into the Danube.

Marlborough had saved the Holy Roman Empire of the Habsburgs and was duly rewarded by the Emperor Leopold, who created him a Prince of the Empire a few weeks after the Battle of Blenheim. The following year he received the Principality of Mindelheim in Swabia from the Emperor Joseph.

In England the news was greeted as the greatest military victory since Agincourt nearly three centuries before. "I have had the happiness of receiving my dear Mr Freeman's by Colonel Parkes, with the good news of this glorious victory, which, next to God Almighty, is wholly owing to dear Mr Freeman, on whose safely I congratulate you with all my soul," Mrs Morley (the Queen) wrote to Mrs Freeman (the Duchess of Marlborough).

For Mr Freeman the battle may have been won but the war was by no means over. It was to drag on for another nine years during which the Duke consolidated his reputation as perhaps the greatest commander of all time, with significant victories at Tirlemont in 1705, Ramillies in 1706, Oudenarde in 1708, Malplaquet in 1709 and finally the capture of Bouchain in 1711. With the benefit of historical hindsight, how much better it would have been if peace terms had been thrashed out not in the unsatisfactory Treaty of Utrecht of 1713, but in the wake of Marlborough's triumphant progress into Brussels in May 1706 following his victory over Marshal Villeroi at Ramillies. To the gossipy Bishop Burnet who asked the Duke the difference between the Battles of Blenheim and Ramillies, Marlborough replied that "the first battle lasted between seven and eight hours and we lost above 12,000 men in it; whereas the second lasted not above two hours and we lost not above 2,500 men."

Another opportunity for peace was missed after the Battle of Oudenarde in 1708 (commemorated in the tapestry in the Third State Room at Blenheim Palace). Here Marlborough and his comrade-in-arms Prince Eugène overwhelmed an enormous French force under the incompetent command of the squabbling Dukes of Vendôme and Burgundy. Fearing a subsequent attack on France, Louis XIV intimated that a peace treaty might be acceptable, only to find the terms offered not to his liking. The next major battle, the bloodbath of Malplaquet in 1709 (shown in one of the tapestries in the First State Room at Blenheim Palace), which counted as an Allied victory even though 18,000 of their men were killed compared with only 11,000 French, served to put back the prospects of peace still further. The French, under Marshal Villars, excelled themselves and took fresh heart. The English, or "British" (bearing in mind the Act of Union a couple of years before), were now tending to think that they had had quite enough of "Marlborough's Wars".

Despite the indifference, or worse, at home to the Duke's last success, the brilliant capture of Bouchain and the penetration of Marshal Villars' much-vaunted *"ne plus ultra"* lines in 1711, meant a great deal to him. He duly added the appropriate tapestries to the sequence woven in Brussels under his careful supervision (they now hang in the Second State Room of Blenheim Palace, while the portrait of the Duke studying a plan of Bouchain is in the Third State Room), though a dog in the foreground appears to have been given horse's hooves.

During his long absences abroad, the Duke's political enemies seemed to believe that he himself had cloven hooves. The trouble was that the Marlboroughs had become entangled in the cross-fire of party politics. Originally a Tory, the Duke, under the influence of his wife, flirted with the Whigs and – rather like his descendant, the late Sir Winston Churchill, two centuries later – ended up being regarded with suspicion by both parties.

The Marlboroughs' problems had been exacerbated by the fiery Sarah's failure to notice the shift in Anne's attitude towards her once she became Queen. To Sarah the two old friends were still plain "Mrs Morley" and "Mrs Freeman", but Queen Anne no longer relished being bossed about by her lady-in-waiting, particularly on political matters. Following the loss of her son in 1703, which coincided with what would now be called her "menopause", Sarah's behaviour towards the Queen became increasingly dictatorial and eccentric.

Basically Sarah was an ardent Whig; Anne a mild Tory. Their political differences – or rather Sarah's refusal to allow any differences from her own point of view – began to create a rift between them. After the triumph of Blenheim, a certain marked coolness was apparent in their relationship when Sarah insulted the Queen's "unfortunate" grandfather, Charles I, from whom she suggested Anne had inherited her persistent prejudice against the Whigs.

From 1707 onwards Sarah became obsessed with the idea that her own poor relation, Abigail Hill (later Lady Masham), whom she had introduced to court, had supplanted her in the Queen's affections. The Marlboroughs became paranoid that "Tricky Robin" Harley, the Tory politician, was using Abigail as his creature with the Queen so as to form an alternative government. "Your Majesty's favour to the Duchess of Marlborough was always looked upon as a peculiar happiness to your people because it naturally led you to put your chief confidence in the two ablest men of your kingdom ... [i.e. Godolphin and Marlborough]," declared Sarah in her most authoritarian manner. "Must she at last be disgraced for the sake of one raised by herself from nothing, one without a character, almost without a name?"

Sarah then went so far as to accuse the Queen of carrying on a homosexual affair with Abigail, and entertained her fellow Whig ladies in their drawing-rooms by singing lewd ditties about "a dirty chamber maid" having "the conduct and the care" of "some dark deeds at night". On the way up the steps to St Paul's Cathedral for a celebration of Marlborough's victory at Oudenarde, an undignified scene took place as Sarah argued violently with the Queen (Anne had apparently failed to wear the jewels Sarah had laid out for her), whom she told to shut up. The quarrels continued – more accusations of lesbianism from Sarah and even a suggestion that the Queen should cease from taking Communion until she had atoned for her maltreatment of her dear friend – as the Duke and Duchess of Marlborough fell irrevocably from favour.

The Duke took particular exception to Anne's demand that he should promote Abigail's brother, Captain Jack Hill, to the rank of Colonel. In January 1710 he wrote to the Queen bewailing the fact that "after all I have done it has not been able to protect me against the malice of a Bedchamber woman", adding that he saw no alternative to offering his resignation. The Queen gave way and the Duke withdrew his resignation, but she blamed the Marlboroughs – unjustly it appears – for the Whigs' demand that Abigail be dismissed from the royal household.

Instead, in 1711, both Sarah and the Duke were themselves dismissed from all their posts. After his great military achievements, to be ruined as a result of a bedchamber wrangle, mixed up with party politics, was a sad end to the Duke's public career. The official grounds for his dismissal were the misappropriation of public funds. A Commission, appointed to examine the public accounts, reported that "among other evidences of corruption and abuse, there was full proof of the Duke having received in the shape of a bribe an annual present of £5,000 or £6,000 from the contractors of bread for the army." The charges against him were not pressed. The legend of Marlborough's meanness and avarice, however, has never died down. "He is as covetous as Hell," wrote Swift, "and as ambitious as the Prince of it." The anecdotes illustrating his extreme carefulness with money are legion. When Lord Peterborough was once mistaken for the Duke of Marlborough by a London crowd ("God bless the Duke of Marlborough"), he hit upon the best way of disabusing them of this idea. "I will give you two convincing proofs that I am not: one is that I have but a single guinea; the other is that I give it to you." Even the late Sir Winston Churchill could not resist re-telling the story of the Duke touching General Pulteney, once his ADC, for sixpence after a game of cards in Bath so that he could take a sedan chair home. Pulteney's brother, Lord Bath, who was of the company, commented "I would venture any sum, now, that the Duke goes home on foot. Do pray follow him out." The General duly did so and was indeed able to witness his old commander tramping back to his lodgings.

Out of office, the Duke should have been able to spend more time inspecting progress on Blenheim Palace, to which his thoughts had often turned during the long years of campaigning. "Pray press on my house and garden," he had urged Sarah, "for I think I shall never stir from my own home." In the event, such was the bitterness between Queen Anne and the Marlboroughs that the Duke felt obliged to travel on the Continent where what he had done to save Europe from the dictatorship of Louis XIV was more appreciated than it seemed to be in England. He was suitably fêted in the courts of the Allies and treated with due deference in his own principality of Mindelheim in Swabia. Ironically, under the terms of the Tory-inspired Treaty of Utrecht of 1713 ending the War of the Spanish Succession, the Duke lost Mindelheim, which was exchanged for the County of Mellenburg (then elevated into a Principality) in Upper Austria by Emperor Charles VI.

The death of Queen Anne in 1714 brought Marlborough back

once more on to the stage of State, if not this time to its centre. In the months before the unhappy, obese and gout-ridden monarch's death, the Duke had been up to his old intrigues. In case the Protestant succession of the House of Hanover to the British throne did not proceed smoothly, he had thought it prudent to renew his Jacobite contacts and asked his nephew, the Duke of Berwick, to secure him a pardon from the "Old Pretender", James II's son and namesake, for the part he had played in deposing his father. As things turned out, he need not have worried, for the first State paper executed by the new King of Great Britain and Ireland, George I, in 1714 reappointed the Duke to his post of Captain-General of the Forces. He was also restored to many of his other positions such as Master-General of the Ordnance, Colonel of the 1st Foot Guards and membership of the Privy Council. His last involvement in military matters was as an adviser during the Jacobite Rebellion of 1715. By now, though, he was no longer up to any active role.

The years were at last beginning to tell on the sexagenarian Duke. "Marlborough has suffered so much," the Imperial Ambassador had noted in 1711, "that he no longer looks like himself." Soon his health, both mental and physical, was to go the way of his looks. In the spring of 1716 his daughter Anne, the second wife of the Whig politician the 3rd Earl of Sunderland (or plain "Mr Charles Spencer" as this near-Republican liked to be referred to), died of pleuritic fever. The loss of another child, to whom he had been particularly close, proved a crippling blow to this always compassionate old soldier. A few weeks later, the Duke had a severe stroke from which he never fully recovered. To those who did not know him he seemed practically an imbecile ("From Marlborough's eyes the tears of dotage flow"), in his last years – much of them spent going from spa to spa. One malicious source, seeing him at Tunbridge Wells, noted that he had been turned into "a mere child and driveller", while "his lady, little concerned, games from morning till night". Such comments were unjust. As Sarah fondly recorded after his eventual death in 1722, "his understanding was as good as ever". He did not speak much to strangers, "because when he was stopt, by not being able to pronounce some words, it made him uneasy. But to his friends that he was used he would talk freely."

Marlborough's memory remained comparatively unimpaired. He could look back on a life in which, as his descendant Sir Winston Churchill proudly claimed, by "his invincible genius in war and his scarcely less admirable qualities of wisdom and management he had completed that glorious process that carried England from her dependency on France to ten years' leadership of Europe." If, as Trevelyan observed, "he loved money, he gave England better value for every guinea he received than any other of her servants."

Towards the end of his days, wandering around the great

rooms in the palace built as a monument to his famous victory at Blenheim, John Churchill, 1st Duke of Marlborough stopped beside a portrait of himself in his prime painted by Sir Godfrey Kneller (which hangs in the Green Writing-Room). He stood in front of the picture, lost in thought. "That," he is said to have observed, "once was a man."

Military mementoes of Marlborough's Wars in a corner of the Great Hall. The ducal standard is on the right of the picture.

41

3. "Strain'd Constructions"

The building of Blenheim Palace remained a source of delight and diversion to the 1st Duke of Marlborough to the end of his life in 1722, even if its long-drawn-out labours became the despair of his Duchess. To Sarah, the Duke's love of Blenheim was his "greatest weakness", but to Jack Churchill, the boy who had never really had a family home, the monumental new palace represented the fulfilment of his dreams. Here was to be a solid, tangible measure of his magnificent achievements and the seat of the dynasty he had raised from obscurity to international fame.

The history of the royal estate which the Duke of Marlborough had been granted by Act of Parliament in 1705 goes back to pre-Conquest days, for King Ethelred the Unready is said to have held a council at Woodstock. The Domesday survey of 1086 refers to the King's vast forests hereabouts and there is evidence that Woodstock became a favourite haunt of William the Conqueror's son, Henry I, who surrounded the park with a stone wall seven miles long. This was to enclose not only the royal deer, but also an exotic menagerie ("lions, leopards, lynxes or camels, animals which England does not produce", according to a contemporary chronicler), thereby providing a respectable precedent for a "safari park" that later owners of the estate have wisely ignored.

Woodstock evolved as an important royal palace in the reign of Henry I's grandson, Henry II, the first monarch of the House of Plantagenet. Above the River Glyme (close to the far side of Vanbrugh's superb bridge which now spans the lake from the Marlboroughs' palace), Henry erected a rambling structure of buildings and courtyards, with an aisled Great Hall. Some pieces of chevron carving from the old palace have been discovered in the rubble filling Vanbrugh's bridge.

Henry also built a remarkable cloistered retreat in the park known as Everswell, planned round a spring from which the water ran through three pools. The exquisite idea of an enclosed garden with chambers and water may have been inspired by the legend of *Tristram and Iseult*. Certainly this romantic spot inspired a legend of its own, for in popular mythology Everswell (or "Rosamond's Well" as it later came to be known) was regarded as the secret bower of the King's mistress, Rosamond Clifford, hidden in a labyrinth of paths. One story goes that Queen Eleanor discovered the bower by following a trail of silk leading to a casket which the King had given "Fair Rosamond". Accord-

Opposite: The south, or garden, front of the palace.

ing to a lurid French chronicler, the Queen then proceeded to strip Miss Clifford, roasted her between two fires and finally bled her to death in a hot bath. Alternative versions give the cause of her demise as stabbing or poisoning. In fact, there is no evidence that Queen Eleanor did murder Rosamond Clifford, who seems to have died of natural causes in Godstow Convent in 1176.

Henry III greatly embellished the palace of Woodstock by adding another handful of chapels, and a suite of royal chambers, adorned with the earliest example of ornamental battlements. It was further improved by, among others, Edward III and Henry VII, whose granddaughter Elizabeth I was later imprisoned by her half-sister Mary Tudor in the gatehouse he had rebuilt. Understandably, after comparing her unwelcome stay there unfavourably with Newgate Gaol, Elizabeth seldom returned to the now decaying palace. After being severely damaged by the Roundheads during a twenty-day siege in 1646, Woodstock Manor, as it was by now known, was well on to the way to becoming a ruin by the time John Vanbrugh, the architect chosen to build Blenheim Palace, surveyed the scene.

Grasping the picturesque potential, Vanbrugh was all in favour of retaining the old royal palace as a feature of his own composition. In his "Reasons Offer'd for Preserving Some Part of the Old Manor", Vanbrugh observed that the venerable buildings would look well from the new palace, affording a view of "One of the Most Agreeable Objects that the best of Landskip Painters could invent". The architect's romanticism was not shared by Sarah or by her friend Sidney Godolphin who remarked that it was a pity the view was spoilt by a pile of ruins. Before he utterly fell out with the tempestuous Sarah, Vanbrugh took it upon himself to reside in the habitable part of the old manor. Today a stone memorial on the site is the only reminder of what Vanbrugh called "the Remains of distant Times".

Vanbrugh, forty-one years old when he received the commission to "erect a large Fabrick at Woodstock", had led a somewhat picaresque life. The grandson of a Protestant émigré from Ghent, one Van Brugg, he was brought up in Chester and commissioned at the age of twenty-two in the infantry. In 1691 he was imprisoned in the Bastille on suspicion of being a spy. Abandoning the military life, "Captain Van" next enjoyed considerable success as a playwright with his Restoration-style comedies, such as *The Relapse* and *The Provok'd Wife*. By the end of the seventeenth century, as Swift noted, we find

> Van's genius, without thought or lecture,
> Is hugely turn'd to architecture.

Although possessed of tremendous style, imagination and bags of confidence, Vanbrugh had little idea of how to put his grandiose ideas on to paper, but in the spring of 1699 he met the perfect collaborator in Nicholas Hawksmoor, the best-trained professional architect of his day, who had studied under Wren. Vanbrugh promptly engaged Hawksmoor as his right-hand man ("organizer, draughtsman and designer") and they worked together on the design of Castle Howard, the 3rd Earl of Carlisle's sublime palace in Yorkshire – a masterpiece bursting with baroque exuberance. Thanks to Lord Carlisle's patronage, Vanbrugh soon replaced William Talman as the Comptroller of His Majesty's works and so the inspired amateur found himself second only to the great Sir Christopher Wren, the King's Surveyor.

The exact circumstances of the Blenheim Palace commission remain extraordinarily hazy, and their very uncertainty gave rise to many of the problems that were to beset its execution. Although Queen Anne obviously undertook to pay for the erection of a suitable structure on the royal estate she granted the Duke of Marlborough in February 1705, there were no terms, conditions or indeed a document of any sort to establish the course of action. According to Vanbrugh, Queen Anne had left the choice of architect to the Duke of Marlborough. According to Sarah, Vanbrugh was appointed by Queen Anne herself.

"I never liked any building so much for the show and vanity of it as for its usefulness and convenience," wrote Sarah later, "and therefore I was always against the whole design of Blenheim, as too big and unwieldy, whether I considered the pleasure of living in it, or the good of my family who were to enjoy it hereafter." Sarah would have preferred Sir Christopher Wren, as she made clear when she commissioned the old master to design her London house on the site of the old friary near St James's Palace in 1709. Marlborough House, she insisted, must be made "strong plain and convenient and that he [Wren] must give me his word that this building should not have the least resemblance of any thing in that called Blenheim which I had never liked but could not prevail against Sir John." (Vanbrugh was knighted by George I in 1714.) In the end, she completed the building under her own direct control; it remained the family's town house until the early nineteenth century.

Queen Anne, in Sarah's version of events, not having "any particular favour for Sir Christopher", opted for Wren's number two at the Board of Works, Vanbrugh, for the building of Blenheim Palace. But Vanbrugh maintains that he accompanied Marlborough down to Woodstock to inspect the site at the direct invitation of the great Duke himself. Not for Marlborough the chaste elegance of Wren, it seems; rather the triumphant, spectacular symbolism of victory that only Vanbrugh's genius could have created.

It was as a monument, not as a dwelling, [wrote his descendant Sir Winston Churchill] that he so earnestly desired it. Hence

the enormous thickness of the walls and masses of masonry in Vanbrugh's plan had appealed to him, and had probably been suggested by him. As the Pharaohs built their pyramids, so he sought a physical monument which would certainly stand, if only as a ruin, for thousands of years. About his achievements he preserved a complete silence, offering neither explanations nor excuses for any of his deeds. His answer was to be this great house.

The Duke knew the architect through their joint membership of the Kit-cat Club, the convivial Whig meeting place off Temple Bar, where "Van" was one of the leading spirits, and they shared an assured aristocratic outlook. As Robert Adam pointed out later in the eighteenth century, Vanbrugh understood better than either Inigo Jones or Christopher Wren "the art of living among the great". As the site of the new palace, Vanbrugh chose a broad plateau at the southern end of Woodstock Park which appealed to his sense of theatre. In front, to the north, was a dramatically steep valley down to the River Glyme, then little more than a brook. On the other side of the valley – in his mind's eye to be approached by a magnificent bridge leading to a grand avenue – were the picturesque ruins of old Woodstock Manor.

Vanbrugh's design for the palace, which had a superficial

similarity to his plan of Castle Howard, provides the main building with wings projecting at right angles, thus forming a forecourt. Behind these wings are situated, to the east and west respectively, the Kitchen and Stable Courts. The main building, the actual house, is set well back from the wings, to which it is joined by colonnades, so as to afford the luxury of having two distinct side "fronts" (east and west), as well as those of the entrance and garden façades (north and south).

The palace was built from east to west. The idea was to insert the private apartments of the Duke and Duchess of Marlborough in the east front (where they are to be found to this day) and create a single large gallery running the length of the west front (now the Library). In between, along the southern, or garden, front, comes the suite of apartments always intended to be used for State or ceremonial purposes rather than for domestic life. The Great Hall, approached through the main entrance, and the Saloon directly behind it, facing out over the Great Parterre (now the south lawn), are the two principal interiors, rising to the full height of the porticoes in the centre of the north and south fronts.

To achieve a symmetrical effect, Vanbrugh employed his favourite trick of placing four massive towers at the corners of the main block. These give the building the look of a fortress rather than a palace and indeed in the early days it was sometimes referred to as "Blenheim Castle". The combination of Classical grace and rugged strength is, as Laurence Whistler has observed, at once Roman and medieval: "the Rome and Middle Ages of the soldier, of hard campaigning and triumphant returns".

Whoever was responsible for choosing him as the architect, Vanbrugh considered Blenheim "much more as an intended Monument of the Queen's glory than a private Habitation for the Duke of Marlborough". He went to considerable pains to show Queen Anne what was being built in her name:

> That the Queen might not be deceiv'd in what she Directed and be afterwards dissatisfyd with it, A very large, Exact, And intelligible Model of the Building was made in Wood and when it was compleated it was set in the Gallery at Kensington by her Order, and there left sometime, that she might Consider it at her leisure, both Alone and with other people ... She Expressed her Self extreamly pleased with it, Shew'd a desire of having it dispatched with all Aplication, and required no sort of Alteration in it.

In fact the model, which, sadly, later disappeared (and should not be confused with those rendered in bamboo and icing-sugar that are currently on display in the Library at Blenheim), differs in several particulars from the finished design. The great portico on the entrance front, for instance, was a later touch.

The application, at least to begin with, proceeded rapidly. After the Act of Parliament which confirmed the Queen's gift of

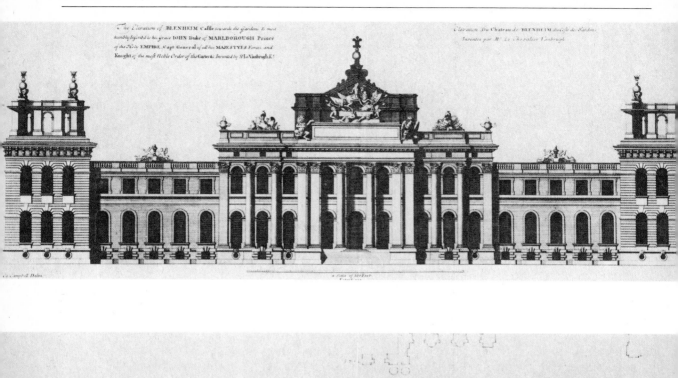

Top: Vanbrugh's plan for the south, or garden, front of the palace. This is how it was built, minus the embellishments of statues and trophies.
Above: An unexecuted plan by Vanbrugh for the same front, featuring Doric columns.

the royal Manor of Woodstock to the Duke of Marlborough at the end of February 1705, the Lord Treasurer, Godolphin, appointed Henry Joynes and William Boulter clerks of works, and they took up residence at Woodstock. Vanbrugh subsequently wondered whether he should not have "some visible Authority likewise, being to act in a Station of much greater Trust". He was accordingly issued with a warrant of appointment as Surveyor, signed by Godolphin in June 1705. Curiously enough, although it was generally accepted that the building was to be a present from the Queen to the Duke of Marlborough and was to be paid for by the government, Godolphin stated that the appointment was being made "for and on behalf of the said Duke". The lack of any sort of financial specifications or clear government directives was, of course, to result in chaos. Relying on a steady supply of government hand-outs, or grants, to pay for the building work was

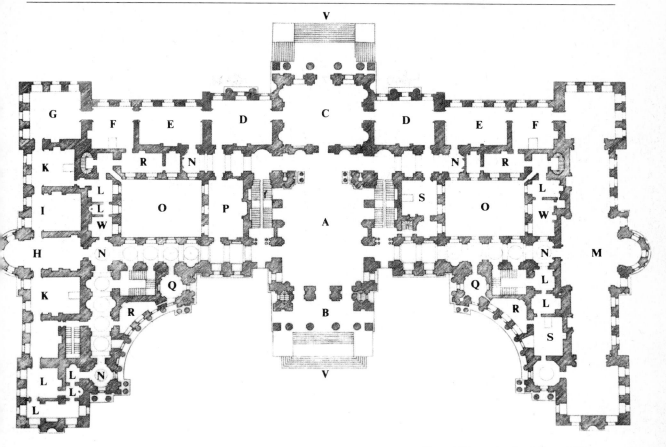

doubtless all very well while the Marlboroughs still basked in royal favour, but it displayed no foresight as to possible future changes.

A few days after his belated official appointment, Vanbrugh was at Woodstock for the ceremonial laying of the foundation stone. A contemporary observer noted:

> About six o'clock in the evening, was laid the first stone of the Duke of Marlborough's house, by Mr Vanbrugge, and then seven gentlemen give it a stroke with a hammer, and threw down each of them a guinea. There were several sorts of musick, three morris dances; one of young fellows, one of maidens, and one of old beldames. There were about a hundred buckets, bowls and pans, filled with wine, punch, cakes and ale. From my lord's house all went to the Town Hall where plenty of sack, claret, cakes, etc, were prepared for the gentry and better sort; and under the Cross eight barrels of ale, with abundance of cakes, were placed for the common people.

One of the "seven gentlemen" who struck the foundation stone was Nicholas Hawksmoor. He was involved in the plans from their outset; as Laurence Whistler has written, "though Blenheim as a whole is Vanbrugh's, yet there is not one detail of

Plan of the principal floor of the palace (as illustrated in Vitruvius Britannicus*). Key:*

A	*Great Hall*
B	*Portico*
C	*Saloon*
D	*Antechamber*
E	*Drawing-Room*
F	*Great Bedchamber*
G	*Grand Cabinet*
H	*Vestibule*
I	*Antechamber*
K	*Bedchamber*
L	*Wardrobe and Closet*
M	*The Great Galley*
N	*Vaulted Corridors*
O	*Little Courts*
P	*Little Dining-Room*
Q	*Lesser Closets*
R	*Dressing-Rooms*
S	*Little Apartments*
T	*Grand Court*
V	*Gardens*
W	*Little Ante- or Waiting-Room*

which one could say with certainty that Hawksmoor had not designed it." Hawksmoor's letters to the two clerks of works, Joynes and Boulter, reveal how much of the organization was indeed his. He advises on such points as how to cover the walls for the winter against frost, on selecting stone of suitable colour and quality, gives directions for measuring the work and on the inescapable matter of money.

Wren, who far from being rejected out of hand continued to act as a sort of consultant to his colleague's ambitious project, reckoned that the cost of building Blenheim would be about £100,000, but this estimate only related to the main block. The sum spent on the initial works in and around the palace, as opposed to later remodellings and renovations, ended up as nearer £300,000, of which £60,000 came from the Marlboroughs themselves and the balance from the government. Vanbrugh boasted to the Duke that "near fifteen hundred" men, excluding the numerous stone-carters, were working on the house when operations started in earnest in the summer of 1705. As far as craftsmen were concerned, it was a case of nothing but the best. Edward Strong senior, fresh from his work at St Paul's Cathedral for Wren, and his son and namesake, John Townsend, Bartholomew Peisley and Henry Banks were the master masons. Grinling Gibbons did most of the stone ornamentation and twenty-two statues. Sir James Thornhill and Louis Laguerre painted ceilings and walls. Langley Bradley made the clock; John Rowley was responsible for the sundials; the Hopsons and the Smallwells did the joinery; Matthew Banks and John Barton undertook the carpentry; Robert Weatherill and, later, Isaac Mansfield, executed the stucco and plastering.

The glories of Blenheim have always extended beyond the stonework and decoration to the gardens and landscapes. Sometimes when a new house is built the design of the gardens is left until later, but Vanbrugh liked everything to happen at once. "The Garden Wall was set agoing the Same day with the House," he reported to the Duke shortly after the foundation ceremony, "and I hope will be done against your Grace's return . . . The Kitchen Garden Walls will likewise be so advanc'd that all the Plantations may be made." Vanbrugh added rashly that "in Generall the Whole Gardens will be form'd and planted in a year from their beginning." His hopes raised, the Duke was soon urging Sarah to check on the progress of Henry Wise, the veteran royal landscape gardener working at Blenheim. He looked forward to the "great pleasure" of seeing "the walks in the park planted". Daniel Defoe relates in his *Journey Through England* (1724) how the 1st Duke of Marlborough had

> Mr Wise consider he was an old man and could not expect to live till the trees were grown up and therefore he expected to have a garden as it were ready made for him. Accordingly Mr

Wise transplanted thither full grown trees in baskets, which he buried in the earth, which look and thrive the same as if they had stood there thirty or forty years.

Although the splendid formal landscape around the palace laid out by Vanbrugh and Wise was "naturalized" by "Capability" Brown when tastes changed later in the eighteenth century, the main axial avenues of trees they planted are still extant. The gardens in the early days had three distinct features – the Great Parterre, the walled Kitchen Garden and the Duchess's formal flower garden – only the second of which survives, as an atmospheric and quite outstanding example of its kind. The red brick walls of the Kitchen Garden were built from 1705 onwards by Richard Stacey and Thomas Churchill (no apparent relation), the bricklayers responsible for Queen Anne's Orangery at Kensington Palace. Within, some eight acres of fruit and vegetables were laid out with military neatness. During his slogging campaigns on the Continent, Marlborough's mind would wander to this enchanted enclosure with its peaches, pears, nectarines and plums. "If you have the same weather, it must make all sortes of fruit very good; and as this is the 3rd yeare of the trees at Woodstock, if possible, I shou'd wish that you might, or somebody you can relie on, taste the fruit of every tree, so that what is not good may be chang'd," he wrote to Sarah in 1707. "On this matter you must advise with Mr Wise, as also what place may be proper for the ice-house; for that shou'd be built this summer, so that it might have time to dry. The Hott weather makes me think of these things, for the most agreeable of all the presents I receive is that of ice." He found the news that the ice-house "can't be of use these three years, is a very melancholy prospect to me, who am turned on the ill side of fifty-seven." The ice-house, situated near the south-eastern boundary of the park, is now no more, having been closed and abandoned some years ago.

Gone, too, is the Great Parterre that used to stretch for half a mile from the south front of the palace; though in present-day heatwaves, when the grass of the south lawn is parched, the original earthwork patterns are visible from a fine vantage point such as the marvellous roofscape or a helicopter. The baking summer of 1976 yielded a fascinating reconstruction of Vanbrugh and Wise's "military" framework of bastions and stone-built curtain walls. The four-sided parterre, well stocked with evergreens from Wise's celebrated London nursery at Brompton (now built over by the museums of South Kensington) and formally laid out to provide walks among ponds and fountains, led to a six-sided formal "wilderness" called the Woodwork.

Duchess Sarah's flower garden, liberally provided with blooms from Wise's London nursery, was where the Italian Garden (created by the 9th Duke of Marlborough) now is, on the east front. It was originally enclosed by Vanbrugh's "out-

Henry Wise, the master of the English formal garden, who laid out the Great Parterre to the south of the palace. Portrait by Kneller.

boundary wall" but as this spoilt Sarah's view from the Bow Window Room (the present dining-room in the private apartments), she insisted that it be removed.

"I have always had the misfortune to suffer very great mischiefs from the assistance of architects," wrote Sarah towards the end of her life. She had a withering contempt for the architects' profession, "knowing of none that are not mad or ridiculous". In her own admission she "made Vanbrugh my enemy by the constant disputes I had with him to prevent his extravagance." The architect was to complain that he was forced into Chancery by "that BBBB old B the Duchess of Marlborough".

From the beginning of building operations at Blenheim, Sarah found plenty to gripe about. The stone quarried from the park proved "extreme bad", causing cracking. As a consequence, some of the walls had to be rebuilt. The haulage of stone from further afield – with over twenty quarries as sources – was a slow and costly process. Even so, by the middle of 1707 the roof was on the eastern range of the main block containing the family apartments and there was confident talk of completion within another couple of years. Sarah even went so far as to say that she would live to beg his pardon for ever having quarrelled with him.

But the truce was only temporary. In 1708 Vanbrugh's repair of parts of old Woodstock Manor, where he fancied he might take up residence himself, infuriated Sarah, who wanted the ruins razed to the ground. The architect was accused of time-wasting, deceit and profligacy. He finally lost the battle to preserve this key feature in the landscape. His cause was not helped by his taking up residence in part of the old manor during the Marlboroughs' absence abroad in 1713. Ironically, the rubble from the demolished building was then used to fill in the Grand Bridge, perhaps Vanbrugh's finest piece of work at Blenheim.

The bridge, begun in 1708 by Peisley under Vanbrugh's supervision, carries the grand approach over the Glyme valley from one side of the hill to the other at a height of some 40 feet above the surface of the present lake. When it was built there was no lake to speak of, merely a marsh. Wren had recommended a bridge only 15 feet high, but Vanbrugh's grandiose scheme, which, as designed, included an arcaded superstructure 80 feet high, held a great appeal for the Duke. Sarah, of course, found it another flagrant example of the architect's extravagance and managed to squash the idea of the arcade atop the bridge. Even without the intended superstructure, the bridge was a very ambitious construction, with four pavilions containing large rooms and a main arch spanning 101 feet. Sarah cuttingly claimed to have counted no less than 33 rooms contained within the bridge; Vanbrugh, in a riposte worthy of one of his plays, said that if Her Grace should find a house inside the bridge she would go and live in it.

As the Marlboroughs fell into increasing bad odour with the

Queen, the government money to pay the building bills was reduced to a trickle moving more slowly than the modest Glyme under Vanbrugh's bridge. The men were simply not being paid, although the work was well advanced – the shell of the main block nearly finished, the famous gilded copper balls present and correct. Matters came to a head in 1710 with the advent of the Tory administration under Harley; Sarah promptly ordered all work to be stopped and had the men laid off. It was feared that the edifice was at an end. Vanbrugh wrote to the Duke: "I shall, notwithstanding all this cruel usage from the Duchess of Marlborough, receive and with pleasure Obey Any Command Your Grace will please to lay upon me."

The immediate problem, in October 1710, was whether the uncovered building would survive the forthcoming winter. Some £200,000 had been spent already, and a further £30,000 was owed to the workmen. Vanbrugh tackled the Tories and the Treasury direct; enough cash was vouchsafed to avert the crisis. "Tricky Robin" Harley seemed sympathetic to the palace's plight, and arranged for work to continue in 1711. Then he pounced: Marlborough was accused of embezzlement and dismissed from all his posts. In June 1712 all building at Blenheim was stopped by the Queen's command; later in the year the Duke and Duchess went into what Sarah described as "a sort of exile".

The deserted, unfinished Blenheim stood, as Vanbrugh observed, "a monument of ingratitude". His loyalty to the Duke cost him dear for, not only was he one of the chief creditors (there were £45,000 worth of debts owed on the building at the time of its abandonment), but he was dismissed from his job with the Board of Works for complaining in a letter to the Mayor of Woodstock of the "persecution" the Duke had suffered. Upon the Marlboroughs' "restoration" in 1714, following the death of Queen Anne and the accession of George I, the Duke ensured that his long-suffering architect was rewarded with a knighthood.

Revisiting Blenheim with Vanbrugh after his return from exile, the Duke said that he intended to finish the building at his own expense, provided the new Whig government would clear the outstanding debts. In the meantime, some of the creditors, such as Strong, had felt obliged to sue the Duke for their money after the Tories had blithely disclaimed any responsibility. Although some funds were eventually forthcoming from the Treasury, it was only a third of what was due; moreover, the Duke himself was not prepared to pay Crown rates for the unfinished work. The master craftsmen who had launched the palace with such enthusiasm and skill did not care for this type of shabby treatment. They liked the idea of carrying on even less when Duchess Sarah took over the reins again following the Duke's illness in 1716. The great names – Hawksmoor, Wise, Gibbons, the Strongs and the rest – fade from the picture.

In November 1716 Sir John Vanbrugh decided that he, too, had had enough. In a memorandum written by the Duchess, he stood accused of having "brought the Duke of Marlb: into this Un-happy difficulty Either to leave the thing Unfinished and by Consequence, useless to him and his Posterity or by finishing it, to distress his Fortune, And deprive his Grandchildren of the Provision he inclin'd to make for them." He responded as follows:

These Papers Madam are so full of Far-fetched Labour'd Accusations, Mistaken Facts, Wrong Inferences, Groundless Jealousies and strain'd Constructions: That I shou'd put a very great affront upon your understanding if I suppos'd it possible you cou'd mean anything in earnest by them; but to put a Stop to my troubling you any more. You have your end Madam, for I will never trouble you more Unless the Duke of Marlborough recovers so far to shelter me from such intolerable Treatment.

And so Blenheim's author disappeared from the greatest stage of all, banned from the premises by the Duchess. Once, during the Duchess's absence, Vanbrugh did see something of his creation but in 1725 he was refused admittance to the park. He died a year later.

"One may find a great deal of Pleasure in building a Palace for another; when one shou'd find very little in living in't ones Self." Thus Vanbrugh himself conceded the point that is always wheeled on against his design for Blenheim. As Dr Abel Evans put it in his well-worn ditty "Upon the Duke of Marlborough's House at Woodstock":

See, sir, here's the grand approach,
This way is for his Grace's coach;
There lies the bridge and here's the clock,
Observe the lion and the cock,
The spacious court, the colonnade,
And mark how wide the hall is made!
The chimneys are so well design'd
They never smoke in any wind.
This gallery's contrived for walking,
The window to retire and talk in;
The council chamber for debate,
And all the rest are rooms of state!"
"Thanks, sir," cried I, "'tis very fine,
But where d'ye sleep, or where d'ye dine?
I find by all you have been telling
That 'tis a house, but not a dwelling.

And yet such petty criticism of the palace's inconvenience is to ignore its ceremonial purpose. The heat of the food (now some-times given too much emphasis, anyway), brought all the way from the Kitchen Court, then mattered less than the fiddle-faddle of State protocol for which the rooms in the centre block were designed. None the less, for all the incomparable grandeur of the exterior, there are those who find Vanbrugh's design for the interior at Blenheim slightly disappointing, save for the Great Hall and the Saloon.

The magnificent 67-foot-high Hall, which has vaulted corridors leading off it to the wings, is notable for stone carvings by Gibbons and others, and for Sir James Thornhill's painted ceiling. Marlborough is depicted kneeling in front of Britannia to whom he appears to be describing the Battle of Blenheim. Thornhill dreamed up the notion of making the Hall into a gigantic guardroom full of arms and armour but the scheme came to nothing. Sir James, who fell foul of Sarah over his fee (she thought his painting "not worth half-a-crown a yard", let alone the twenty-five shillings he charged), was also to have painted the Saloon beyond, but lost the job to Louis Laguerre. The Frenchman charged £500 for the murals and ceiling, portraying himself beside Dean Jones, the Duke's chaplain and "sacred domestic", whom the Duchess did not like, but put up with for a time on account of his sharing her fondness for cards. Only one of the four marble doorcases in the Saloon was completed by Grinling Gibbons before the shutdown in 1712: the master carver did not return.

As his parting shot to the Duchess in 1716, Vanbrugh expressed the hope "that your Grace having like the Queen thought fit to get rid of a faithfull servant, the Torys will have the pleasure to see your Glassmaker, Moor, make just such an end of the Duke's Building as her Minister Harley did of his victories for which it was erected." This "Moor" was James Moore, in fact a talented cabinet-maker, whom Sarah appointed her clerk of works in the wake of the mass exodus at the end of 1716. At this juncture the situation was as follows: outside more or less in good shape (though the west, or Stable Court, was never completed); inside anything but. The Bow Window Room in the east wing was without a floor; the State apartments beyond the Saloon and Gallery in the west wing also had a long way to go. The Chapel was "three foot high" according to Sarah's annotated plan of the time, while the Plymouth Moor stone intended for the steps to the north and south fronts had not turned up. Thus, after a dozen years the dream house of the Duke was still not habitable.

For her ailing husband's sake, Sarah determined to press on with all haste to save Blenheim from becoming purely a memorial. In 1719 they were finally able to move into the eastern part of the palace where their two suites (his chambers on the south side, hers on the north) converged on Sarah's beloved Bow Window Room. Then a sitting-room; this was the setting for a performance by the Marlboroughs' grandchildren of Dryden's *All for Love* which succeeded in reviving the old Duke. He was to

The funeral procession of the 1st Duke of Marlborough in London, 9 August 1722. He had directed in his will that he should be buried in the Chapel at Blenheim, but as this building was still unfinished, the corpse of the great soldier found temporary refuge in the Duke of Ormonde's vault at Westminster Abbey. Marlborough was finally laid to rest at Blenheim beside his wife after her death in 1744.

spend just two summers at Blenheim before dying at Windsor on 16 June 1722.

As the Blenheim Chapel was not yet finished, the Duke's funeral took place in Westminster Abbey, although his body was finally brought back to Blenheim after Sarah's death, twenty-two years later. The marble tomb, designed by William Kent and executed by Rysbrack, repeats the theme of the Blenheim Tapestry (Marshal Tallard's surrender to the Duke). The overwhelming memorial above shows Marlborough in his customary symbolic Roman attire with a worshipping Sarah and their two sons, both of whom died young. Like many married couples, the Marlboroughs had lived only for each other, developing, as Peter Quennell has suggested "a kind of *egoism-à-deux* that was apt to preclude any real sympathy with their fellow human beings". Sarah's relationship with her daughters (not even mentioned on the memorial) degenerated into bitterness. Sarah herself later recalled that when she entered the room at Windsor where the Duke was dying, her two surviving daughters, Henrietta Godolphin and Mary Montagu both, "rose up and made curtsies but did not speak to me".

The elder surviving daughter Henrietta, Countess of Godolphin, succeeded to her father's dukedom under the Act of Parliament of 1706 that had broadened its descent to his daughters, but she never lived at Blenheim which remained under the sway of her formidable mother. For Henrietta life certainly began at forty: she became a Duchess in her own right and pregnant by her adulterous idol William Congreve, with whom she kicked over the traces while he was nursing his gout at Bath. After the playwright had died in 1728 from injuries sustained in a coach accident, Henrietta, in the words of Horace Walpole, "exposed herself by placing a monument and silly epitaph of her own composition and bad spelling to Congreve in Westminster Abbey." She too was buried at the Abbey five years later, stipulating in her will that her body "be not at any time hereafter or on any pretence whatsoever carried to Blenham [sic]".

Duchess Henrietta's only son and heir, the feckless William Godolphin, styled Marquess of Blandford by courtesy and known as "Willigo", had predeceased her by a couple of years, probably as a result of a drinking bout. "His only fault," noted the Earl of Egmont in his diary, "was drinking, and loving low company." His wife, a burgomaster's daughter from Utrecht, was some years older than him and, perhaps fortunately, there were no children of the marriage. According to the acidulous Lord Hervey, Duchess Henrietta felt that "anybody who had any regard to *Papa's* memory must be glad that the Duke of Marlborough was now not in danger of being represented in the next generation by one who must have brought any name he bore into contempt."

While the Marlborough succession staggered off to this unpropitious start, Sarah continued her nobly self-sacrificing task of completing what now really had become her husband's memorial. Before the Duke died, however, Sarah had decided to wreak revenge on the architectural profession and building trade in her own inimitable manner by suing 401 people who had been connected in some way or other with work on the palace. These "confederates", all named, from Vanbrugh to the humblest labourer, were accused of having plotted together "to load the Duke of Marlborough with ye payment of the debts due on account of ye Building before her late Majesty putt a Stop thereto", and of charging "excessive and unreasonable rates and prices for the same". To turn on craftsmen who had done their job in good faith, for which they had been paid disgracefully late, if at all; to blame them for an idiotic muddle in one's own sphere of influence and then to accuse them of a conspiracy to defraud must surely rank as the least endearing of this termagant's many disobliging acts. Extraordinarily, this monstrous lawsuit was more or less upheld by Lord Macclesfield, although it may have been no coincidence that this corrupt Lord Chancellor was impeached shortly afterwards for bribery and embezzlement.

Charles Spencer, 3rd Earl of Sunderland, the collector of the celebrated "Sunderland Library", which he mortgaged to his father-in-law, the 1st Duke of Marlborough. His son and namesake became the 3rd Duke of Marlborough in 1733.

Among the defendants was Nicholas Hawksmoor, who, apart from this blanket coverage, had hitherto managed to avoid any direct unpleasantness with the fire-eating Duchess. Doubtless finding that she could no longer manage without his skills, Sarah summoned Hawksmoor in 1722 to resume his connection with Blenheim after half-a-dozen years' absence. Having "always had the greatest affection and regard imaginable for Blenheim", and "wishing to know in what manner the undertaker will finish this work least I should be quite disappointed (when it is done) in the thoughts I conceived of it", Hawksmoor duly complied. Back in the saddle, he produced designs for the Triumphal Arch at the town entrance to the park from Woodstock, for the decoration of the Chapel and the Gallery (then still unfinished), for several ceilings in the house and for obelisks and columns.

The Gallery (now the Long Library) had been planned by Vanbrugh as "a noble room of parade" to fill the west side of the palace. The original idea was for the vast room, 180 feet long and 32 feet high, to be a picture gallery with a painted ceiling by Thornhill. But after the Duchess's wrangles over the cost of the ceilings in the Great Hall and the Saloon, she decided she had had enough of painting. The decoration was accordingly arranged to be stucco and the room was finished as a library, complete with covered bookcases, to house the books of the Duchess's son-in-law, the 3rd Earl of Sunderland. The "Sunderland Library" had been lavishly put together by the scholarly Charles Spencer since his teens to form one of the greatest collections of books ever assembled. Later financial exigencies had compelled Lord Sunderland to mortgage the library to his father-in-law. In the late nineteenth century, the 8th Duke of Marlborough was to sell the Sunderland Library and to convert the room into a picture gallery; the present appearance of the "Long Library", with bookcases replaced, was the work of his son, the 9th Duke.

Hawksmoor's task in the Gallery, or Library, was to design an interior for an existing shell. Faced with a room divided up into five sections, he turned this to his advantage by treating them as five separate compartments. As Hawksmoor's biographer, Kerry Downes, has observed: "The visitor is most conscious of the extent of the room when he walks from end to end, but even then he experiences a sequence of rooms rather than a single long one." Hawksmoor himself refers to the end sections in his notes as "that Salon in ye Gallery next to ye great Court", and 'ye Cabinet of ye Gallery". The ceiling, which has two false domes, was covered in luscious plasterwork by Isaac Mansfield, while William Townsend and Batholomew Peisley executed the white marble pilasters and doorcases. In Professor Downes's authoritative view, the Long Library at Blenheim is perhaps Hawksmoor's finest room. It certainly makes a most refreshing climax to the visitors' tour of the State apartments.

The ceilings of the three rooms to the east of the Saloon – the Green Drawing-Room, the Red Drawing-Room and the Green Writing-Room – have also been firmly attributed to Hawksmoor. His design for these ceilings was an innovative combination of coving and banding, resulting in a powerful effect of height and might that even the 9th Duke's unwise titivation cannot take away. These unnecessary embellishments – almost literally a case of gilding the lily – were, he himself later realized to his chagrin, one of the restoring Duke's few false moves at Blenheim.

Outside in the park, Hawksmoor worked on plans for gate-ways and monuments, though only one of them, the Triumphal Arch or Woodstock Gate came to fruition. The design, with its dramatic echoes of Imperial Rome, was executed by Townsend and Peisley in 1723. The flanking doorways were placed here later in the eighteenth century; like the monumental gatepiers similarly shifted, at about the same time, to form the entrance at the Hensington Gate, they had been designed by Hawksmoor much earlier, and were built as part of the ill-fated garden wall on the east side of the palace. Today the Hensington Gate to the east, off the Oxford Road, is perhaps the most familiar entrance to Blenheim, but the Triumphal Arch reached through the town of Woodstock achieves the consummate *coup de théâtre*. Past the mid-eighteenth-century Town Hall (designed by Sir William Chambers) and the Bear Inn, one comes to a sort of courtyard. It seems like a cul-de-sac but there beyond the Triumphal Arch comes the breathtaking surprise.

In the original scheme of things, however, the main entrance was to be neither of these approaches, but the Ditchley Gate at the north end of the Great Avenue. The grand approach was conceived as being down the two-mile avenue, across the Bridge and Causeway, and up into the Great Court, or North Forecourt. Unfortunately, as the north entrance does not really lead any-where, it has never fulfilled its intended role – though it has recently come into its own as the present Duke's private entrance and exit, being handily placed for his secondary seat, Lee Place at Charlbury to the north-west of Blenheim. After the completion of the more convenient town entrance, Hawksmoor produced suit-ably grandiose designs for the Ditchley Gate, but none of them was adopted by the Duchess, whose enthusiasm for outbuild-ings was never strong. Eventually a considerably more modest design, attributed to a pupil of Chambers's, John Yenn (also responsible for the Temple of Health, built in the pleasure grounds to the south-east of Blenheim Palace to mark one of George III's temporary recoveries from insanity), was erected in 1781 to form the present Ditchley Gate.

The one structure in the park that absorbed Sarah's attention after the Duke's death was the Column of Victory. While her husband was alive she had contemptuously dismissed Van-brugh's typically romantic idea of placing an obelisk alluding to what he called Henry II's "Scenes of Love" near the site of old Woodstock Manor: "If there were obelisks to bee made of what all our Kings have done of that sort," snorted Sarah, "the countrey would be Stuffed with very odd things." Hawksmoor came up with some more purposeful ideas for a memorial to the Duke in his paper, "Explanation of the Obelisk" (*c.* 1724); his designs recalled Trajan's Column in Rome and the Monument to the Fire of London, an early work by his old master Wren. As to its position, Hawksmoor suggested the point where, in present-day terms, the east avenue from the Hensington Gate meets the drive from the Triumphal Arch in front of the East Gate. Although an inscription regarding the building of the palace ("under the auspices of a munificent sovereign this house was built for John Duke of Marlborough, and his Duchess Sarah . . .") was to be placed on the East Gate leading to the Kitchen Court, the Column of Victory itself was finally erected at the beginning of the Great Avenue.

Hawksmoor's labours were characteristically set aside by Sarah and in 1731 the old architect went along to see the result of the substitute design for himself. "The Historicall pillar is set up in the park: (conducted by my Ld Herbert) it is of 10f diameter and in all above 100f high," he wrote to his patron Lord Carlisle at Castle Howard. "I must observe to you, that ye inscription is very long and contains many letters, but tho' they are very legible, they are but three quarters of an Inch high." The "Lord Herbert" he refers to was soon to become the 9th Earl of Pembroke, best remembered for his building of the exquisite Palladian bridge at his seat in Wiltshire, Wilton House. The "Architect Earl" operated in collaboration with his clerk of works Roger Morris, who was also responsible for building the stables (generally regarded as superior to the house) at Althorp in Northamptonshire for Sarah's grandson, Charles Spencer, 5th Earl of Sunderland. As built, the Marlborough monument, sculpted in lead by one Robert Pit, depicts the Duke with eagles at his feet holding a winged Victory atop a Doric column. On the side of the base facing the palace is inscribed a panegyric, with the other sides given over to tedious passages from the Acts of Parliament settling the estate on the Churchills and their descendants in the female line.

The panegyric, the long inscription described by Hawksmoor, had greatly exercised Sarah. "If I should have a mind to expose the ingratitude even of those who reaped the advantages of these successes," she wrote while deliberating how best to record her husband's triumphs, "the whole park and gardens would not hold pillars sufficient to contain the infamy of that relation." After toying with various unsatisfactory versions by divers hands, Sarah swallowed her pride and accepted that the only contemporary capable of commemorating the great Duke was the Marlboroughs' hated political foe from the days of Queen

Anne, Henry St John, Viscount Bolingbroke. Recalling his early admiration for the victor of Blenheim, Lord Bolingbroke rose to the occasion with what Sir Winston Churchill was to describe as "a masterpiece of compact and majestic statement . . . it would serve as a history in itself, were all other records lost." Sarah found the lapidary epitaph by the man who had been responsible with Harley for her husband's eclipse, "the finest thing that was possible for any man to write and as often as I have read it I still wet the paper . . .".

Not only the Column of Victory eluded Hawksmoor, but also the monument to the 1st Duke in the Chapel. Although the original Chapel (later altered in the nineteenth century) was probably decorated largely from his designs once the Gallery, or Library, was finished, the dominant feature, the tomb, was assigned to the team that had recently been commissioned to commemorate the scientist Isaac Newton in Westminster Abbey, William Kent and Michael Rysbrack. Hawksmoor had designed a monument in proportion to its comparatively modest surroundings, whereas the newly-fashionable Kent would appear to have been thinking in the context of a cathedral.

In May 1732 Sarah reported with pride:

> The Chappel is finish'd and more than half the Tomb there ready to set up all in Marble Decorations of Figures, Trophies, Medals with their inscriptions and in short everything that could do the Duke of Marlborough Honour and Justice. This is all upon the Wall of one side the Chappel. And considering how many Wonderful Figures and Whirligigs I have seen Architects finish a Chappel withal, that are of no Manner of Use but to laught at, I must confess I cannot help thinking that what I have designed for this Chappel may as reasonably be call'd finishing of it, as the Pews and Pulpit.

In the memorial mood of the 1730s, Sarah also commissioned Rysbrack to sculpt a white marble bust of the Duke and even "a fine statue" of Blenheim's benefactor, Queen Anne. Sarah took "satisfaction in showing this respect to her, because her kindness to me was real". Such magnanimity was, however, tempered by the Duchess's customary desire for "a bargain" with the sculptor. The Queen's statue, which cost her £300, originally stood in the central apse of the Library (where Rysbrack's bust of the Duke is now), but today it faces down the long room from the south.

Rysbrack also produced a bust of Sarah's son-in-law, Charles Spencer, 3rd Earl of Sunderland, the statesman and bibliophile who had died a few weeks after the 1st Duke of Marlborough in 1722, leaving his orphaned children in the care of their formidable grandmother. Robert, the eldest son and 4th Earl of Sunderland, died in 1729 and so Charles, the 5th Earl, became the heir to the dukedom of Marlborough held by Henrietta following

Rysbrack's statue of Queen Anne in white marble, commissioned by Sarah, Duchess of Marlborough, in indulgent old age, with its "proper inscription". The munificent sovereign now faces down the Long Library.

Lady Diana Spencer Youngest Daughter to Charles 3d. Earl of Sunderland by Lady Ann Churchill his Wife 2d. Daughter to John Duke of Marlborough.

"Lady Di" Spencer was the favourite granddaughter of Sarah, Duchess of Marlborough. Like her present-day collateral niece and namesake, Lady Di seemed destined to marry the Prince of Wales; but, in the event, she married the 4th Duke of Bedford instead.

the death in 1731 of her own wretched son "Willigo". Sarah's relationships with her grandchildren were not much easier, on the whole, than they had been with her daughters. When, at a dinner to celebrate her seventieth birthday she likened the family to a great tree with all its branches flourishing about her, Charles was overheard to murmur, "branches flourish better when their roots are buried." His sister Anne, Lady Bateman, was blamed by their grandmother for introducing Charles to his future wife, Elizabeth Trevor, daughter of one of the 1st Duke's old Tory opponents. The furious Sarah took out her feelings with some graffiti on Anne's portrait: "She is blacker within."

Sarah's two favourite grandchildren were the younger Spencers, Diana and John. "The person, the merit and the family of Lady Diana Spencer are objects so valuable that they must necessarily have ... caused many such applications of this nature to Your Grace," wrote one unsuccessful suitor, the 4th Earl of Chesterfield, to Sarah. But the Duchess had other ideas. For her beloved "Lady Di" (a diminutive in which she rejoiced, unlike her collateral niece and namesake, the present Princess of Wales), Sarah had the then Prince of Wales, George II's unsatisfactory son "Poor Fred", in her sights. All went well until the match was frustrated by Sir Robert Walpole (himself an ancestor, incidentally, of the later Lady Diana), who preferred the prospect of a European match. Instead, Lady Di became the *châtelaine* of Woburn Abbey as the wife of the 4th Duke of Bedford, but died of consumption aged only twenty-six. "Johnnie" Spencer also died at a comparatively young age, although not before he had inherited all his grandmother's personal property.

In old age Sarah found consolation in her dogs:

> They have all of them gratitude, wit, and good sense: things very rare to be found in this country. They are fond of going out with me; but when I reason with them, and tell them it is not proper, they submit, and watch for my coming home, and meet me with as much joy as if I had never given them good advice.

At the age of eighty she dictated an inventory of Blenheim, displaying her extraordinary powers of recall and mastery of practical detail. Thus, as well as notes on the pictures (such as Van Dyck's famous equestrian portrait of Charles I, then hanging where the organ now stands in the Long Library, and now in the National Gallery) and the furnishings, Sarah was able to rattle off that there were 809 napkins, 93 table-cloths, 18 pairs of fine sheets, 45 pairs of servants' sheets, and so forth. Shortly before her eventual death in 1744, she willed that the palace was on no account to be denuded of its contents.

And so Sarah was duly buried beside her husband in the Chapel, following a funeral in keeping with her parsimonious tastes ("without Plumes or Escutcheons"). Whatever her shortcomings, "her with the fury face and fairy heart" was entitled to take pride in having more or less finished the job. Although she would never have admitted to it, one suspects that the old battle-axe may even have become rather fond of Blenheim by the end.

J. Reynolds Pinx^t 1758.   R. Houston Fecit.

His Grace Charles Spencer, Duke of Marlborough,
Master General of the Ordnance, General -in Chief of His Majesty's Foot Forces,
Knight of y^e most Noble Order of y^e Garter, & one of his Maj^{ties} most hon^{ble} Privy Council &c.

Done from a Picture in the Possession of the R^t Hon. the Earl of Pembroke; to whom this Plate, is
most humbly Inscribed by His most Dutiful and Obedient Servant — Rich^d. Houston.

Sold by R. Houston, Charing Cross. Price 2.

4. The results of extravagance

Blenheim had remained Duchess Sarah's for life and neither of her husband's initial successors to the dukedom showed any inclination to move into the palace before her death in 1744. Eleven years previously her grandson Charles, 5th Earl of Sunderland, had succeeded her eldest daughter Henrietta to become the 3rd Duke of Marlborough. All subsequent Dukes of Marlborough descend in the male line from this Spencer heir, whose mother, Anne, had been a Churchill.

The Dukes of Marlborough continued to bear the surname of Spencer alone until 1817, in the patriotic atmosphere after Waterloo, when the 5th Duke assumed the additional surname of Churchill to commemorate his famous ancestor. The present Duke of Marlborough, whose subsidiary titles include the earldom of Sunderland (hence the family diminutive "Sunny") and the barony of Spencer, is indeed the head of the Spencer family. The Althorp branch descend from Johnnie Spencer, to whom this property in Northamptonshire passed after his elder brother Charles inherited the dukedom of Marlborough. Johnnie's son and namesake, a connoisseur who built Spencer House in St James's, was created Earl Spencer in 1765.

The Spencers are a comparatively "new" family among the British aristocracy. Discounting the tenuous claims of ancestry from the medieval Despensers, the pedigree effectively begins with Sir John Spencer, a shrewd Warwickshire sheep-farmer who bought the Althorp estate in Northamptonshire early in the sixteenth century. "My Lord, when these things were doing your ancestors were keeping sheep," said the Earl of Arundel to the 1st Lord Spencer during a Parliamentary debate in 1621; to which Lord Spencer riposted: "When my ancestors were keeping sheep, Your Lordship's ancestors were plotting treason." The 1st Lord Spencer was reputed to have more ready money than anyone else in the kingdom, thanks to his 19,000 sheep and to his cunning deals in cattle, rye and barley. Along with the practical approach of the sheep-farmer, the Spencers have a strong artistic strain: the 2nd Lord Spencer's wife was the daughter of Shakespeare's patron, the Earl of Southampton, and their eldest son, Henry, married the poet Waller's "Sacharissa", Lady Dorothy Sidney. The Cavalier Henry lent £10,000 to Charles I at the beginning of the Civil War and was created Earl of Sunderland in 1643, only to be killed a few months later, aged twenty-three, at the Battle of Newbury.

Opposite: Charles, 3rd Duke of Marlborough, the first "Spencer Duke" from whom all subsequent Dukes of Marlborough descend. He is seen wearing the star and sash of the Order of the Garter.

Above: Sir John Vanbrugh, Blenheim's architect.
This portrait was painted about 1718, not long after
he severed his connection with his great creation
and its turbulent châtelaine ("You have your end
Madam . . .").

Opposite (above): The bridge as it looks today.
Opposite (below): A painting showing Vanbrugh's
Grand Bridge as it was before Capability Brown
created the lakes in the 1760s.

Henry's son, the 2nd Earl of Sunderland, is pithily summed up in the *Dictionary of National Biography* as "the craftiest, most rapacious, and most unscrupulous of all the politicians of his age". The almost equally devious 3rd Earl had, in Sir Winston Churchill's view, "none of the insinuating charm and genial courtesy of his incomprehensible father". His political career finally blew up after his involvement in the financial scandal known as the "South Sea Bubble". Anne Churchill was his second wife and after her death in 1716 he married a third time — much to the annoyance of Sarah, who considered his new bride, apart from her other shortcomings, to have "somewhat of a squint look".

Sarah was even more prejudiced against the wife of her grandson Charles, the eventual 3rd Duke of Marlborough. "The woman herself (as they say, for I have never seen her)," wrote Sarah, "has been bred in a very low way and don't know how to behave herself upon any occasion; not at all pretty, and has a mean, ordinary look. As to the behaviour, if she has any sense, that may mend. But they say she has very bad teeth, which I think is an objection alone in a wife, and they will be sure to grow worse with her time." Miss Trevor's gravest fault, in Sarah's eyes, was lack of money.

The 3rd Duke of Marlborough has been portrayed as rather a dim figure. According to Horace Walpole, he "had virtues and sense enough to deserve esteem, but always lost it by forfeiting respect. He was honest and generous, capable of giving the most judicious advice and of following the worst." The 1st Marquess of Lansdowne described the Duke as an "easy, good-natured gallant man, who took a strange fancy for serving, to get rid of the *ennui* attending a private life, without any military experience or the common habits of a man of business, or indeed capacity for either, and no force of character whatever". None the less, his career in public life seems to have been distinguished enough, with stints as Lord Steward of the Household, Lord Privy Seal and finally in his grandfather's old job of Master General of the Ordnance. As a soldier he apparently did well at the Battle of Dettingen in 1743, being made a Knight Banneret on the field by George II, whose gallant leadership on this last occasion when a monarch led his troops into battle, was somewhat marred by his horse bolting.

In building and decorative terms, there is almost nothing to show at Blenheim for the 3rd Duke of Marlborough's intermittent spells in residence after the death of his grandmother. A vast canvas by Thomas Hudson that he commissioned a couple of years before his death in 1758, which now hangs next to the main staircase at Blenheim, shows the rather podgy Duke with his Duchess and their brood. The Duke died on campaign in Germany soon after his appointment as Commander of the British forces there. The news caused a certain melancholy among his rather too-numerous creditors – as the following couplet recorded:

> They may be false who languish and complain,
> But they who sigh for money never feign

After his death, Duchess Elizabeth apparently made unsuccessful advances to their sons' tutor, John Moore (who later became Archbishop of Canterbury). Her elder daughter, Diana, married Dr Johnson's friend Topham Beauclerk following her divorce from her first husband, Henry St John's nephew, Lord Bolingbroke. The younger daughter, Betty, married the 10th Earl of Pembroke, son of the "Architect Earl" who had "conducted" the Column of Victory in the park at Blenheim. George, the eldest of the 3rd Duke's three sons, succeeded to the dukedom at the age of nineteen and was to "reign" at Blenheim Palace for nearly sixty years.

Under his ownership Blenheim burgeoned and effectively came into its own for the first time as a family seat. An army officer when he inherited the title (he was commissioned in the Coldstream Guards after leaving Eton), the 4th Duke did not pursue a military career, preferring at an early age to exercise his considerable talents in public life. As a follower of Grenville, the Whig leader, he became a Privy Councillor and Lord Chamberlain of George III's household when he was only twenty-three, going on to be Lord Privy Seal the following year. According to one diarist, the Duke was "nervous in the extreme and reserved" though he possessed "a great deal of humour". *The Complete English Peerage* of 1775 describes him as "a nobleman of great worth, generous, humane and hospitable, no abject courtier, yet a lover of peace and an enemy to faction". Seven years later a book called *Ways and Means*, which generally gives unfavourable accounts of public characters, praised him for "Probity and disinterested justice in public life, benevolence and conjugal affection in domestic retirement". By 1792 *The Jockey Club* was castigating him for "an uniform hauteur of deportment", being "sullen and overbearing in his general demeanour". The "domestic retirement" referred to in *Ways and Means* seems to have been his ultimate undoing, for the able politician and scholar, who was a Fellow of the Royal Society, President of the Royal Institution and a Trustee of the British Museum, during the last years of his life became an embittered recluse in the palace he did so much to embellish.

As a young man the highly-strung Duke George was regarded as the greatest "catch" in England after George III. Both Georges were in the sights of the glamorous Lady Sarah Lennox, daughter of the 2nd Duke of Richmond. Prevented from marrying Sarah for political reasons, George III (then a surprisingly romantic figure) is supposed to have written the song about *The Lass of Richmond Hill* ("I'd crowns resign/To call thee mine . . ."). Lady

Within the portrait, inscribed text reads:

SARAH DAUGHTER AND HEIRESS
OF RICHARD IENNINGS OF SANDRIDGE
IN THE COUNTY OF HERTFORD ESQ.
WIFE OF IOHN CHURCHILL
DUKE OF MARLBOROUGH

Sarah, Duchess of Marlborough by Sir Godfrey Kneller. This portrait, which hangs in the Green Drawing-Room at Blenheim, shows Sarah (wearing a mantilla), possibly in mourning for her baby son, Charles.

Lady Henrietta Churchill eldest
Daughter to John Duke of Marlboro
is Wife to Francis Earl of Godolphin

*Another Kneller portrait of Sarah's eldest daughter, Henrietta, who
married Francis, 2nd Earl of Godolphin and succeeded to the dukedom
of Marlborough in 1722.*

71

Sarah then turned her attentions to the other George but as her sister noted: "Alas, alas, the Duke of Marlborough saw Sarah at Ranelagh, took no notice of her and walked all night with Lady Caroline Russell." Lady Caroline was the daughter of the Duke's uncle and guardian, the 4th Duke of Bedford (widower of the ill-fated first "Lady Di" Spencer) by his proud and pushy second wife Lady Gertrude Leveson-Gower, who was set on this illustrious match. Both Lady Sarah and Lady Caroline were to the fore as bridesmaids to George III's monkey-faced German bride Charlotte of Mecklenburg-Strelitz in 1761, but the following year it was Caroline who became the *châtelaine* of Blenheim. The marriage, of nearly half-a-century's duration, was a happy one, though Caroline grew into an even haughtier and less sympathetic character than her mother. Queen Charlotte pronounced the Duchess of Marlborough the proudest woman in England.

The 4th Duke and his family were painted in a grandiose group, complete with two Blenheim spaniels and a whippet, by Sir Joshua Reynolds in 1778. In the impressive canvas, now hung opposite Sargent's group of the 9th Duke and his family in the Red Drawing-Room at Blenheim, the connoisseur 4th Duke is shown in his Garter robes holding one of his sardonyx collection. His heir, the Marquess of Blandford (later the 5th Duke) grasps a box containing some of the Marlborough Gems, while the elder girls are depicted teasing, with the aid of a mask, their little sister Lady Anne (who had declared to Sir Joshua "I won't be painted!"). Reynolds apparently kept his mind on his work by inhaling snuff and when the Duchess, noticing the quantities of the substance that were landing on the carpet, sent for a footman to clear it up, the artist is supposed to have said: "Go away, the dust you make will do more harm to my picture than my snuff to the carpet."

The Duchess once complained that life at Blenheim was *"ennui"* itself, but in the halcyon days before the Duke, an ardent astronomer, decided to withdraw more or less completely to his observatory, there appear to have been plenty of distractions. The Orangery, on the east side of the palace, was converted into a stylish private theatre with seating for two to three hundred people. The audiences were drawn from the county neighbours and the "town and gown" of Oxford and among the casts of amateurs joining the Spencer children to perform was the impecunious historian, the Reverend Edward Nares, who later eloped with one of the Duke's daughters, Lady Charlotte Spencer. The disapproving Duchess continued the unfortunate family tradition of falling out with the next generation by banning Charlotte and her husband from Blenheim.

In happier times each of the Duchess's eight deliveries of babies was celebrated in regal style. For example, the birth of the second son, ancestor of the Viscounts Churchill, was marked by a gargantuan supper of roast beef, mutton and pork, loin and fillet of veal, pork and mutton pies, chicken, ducks, geese, tongues, boar's head, two dishes of soused herrings, an apple pie and two plum puddings. In the summer of 1786 King George III and Queen Charlotte came for the day. "Considering the shortness of the notice," the Duchess wrote to the Marlboroughs' old tutor, the Archbishop of Canterbury, "it all went off very well." She told the Archbishop:

> They stayed here from eleven till six. We had breakfast for them in the library and, after they returned from seeing the park, some cold meats and fruit. Lord and Lady Harcourt told us we were to sit as lord and lady of the bedchamber all the time they stayed here; and poor Lord Harcourt seemed quite happy to rest himself; the Duke found him sitting down behind every door where he could be concealed from royal eyes. We were just an hour going over the principal floor, as they stopped and examined *everything in every room*; and we never sat down during that hour nor indeed very little but while we were in the carriages; which fatigued me more than anything else. Lord Harcourt told the Duke that he had been full-dressed in a bag and sword every morning since Saturday; but the Duke could not follow his example in that, as he had no dress-coat or sword in the country. He desires me to tell you he had no misgivings. All the apprehensions were on my side. Nobody could do the thing better or more thoroughly than he did.

As a reward for his hospitality, the Duke received a Herschel telescope from the King. It was during the royal visit that George III made his celebrated and very apposite comment: "We have nothing to equal this." The 4th Duke, once described by a firm of upholsterers as "a patron ever willing to promote Industry and Ingenuity", had indeed beautified Blenheim both inside and out with the magnificent help of Sir William Chambers and Lancelot ("Capability") Brown. Sir William Chambers, best known as the architect of Somerset House and the designer of the Royal State Coach (still in use), was much admired by George III to whom he had given lessons in architecture when he was Prince of Wales. At Blenheim his works included the prettifying of Vanbrugh's rather forbidding East Gate (now known as the Flagstaff Lodge, through which members of the public obtain access to the palace today); the redecoration of some of the rooms, notably the Duke's Grand "Cabinet" containing some of the Old Masters and other treasures in the south-east tower; and the exquisite New Bridge over the Glyme on the Bladon side of the park. Together with his considerably less talented assistant, John Yenn, Sir William was also responsible for the little Temples of Flora, Diana, and Health (built in honour of one of George III's temporary "recoveries") dotted about the grounds. In the west wall of the Kitchen Garden, Chambers inserted a Palladian

Sir William Chambers, the architect brought in by the 4th Duke of Marlborough to embellish Blenheim in the 1760s. Portrait by Sir Joshua Reynolds.

Left: A bird's eye view of the Great Duke, cast in lead by Robert Pit and attired as a Roman General, atop the 134-foot Doric "Column of Victory" in the park.

Below: Stone carvings on the roof of the Chapel Colonnade by the great Grinling Gibbons, who worked at Blenheim until 1712. Note the military detail — standards, drums, armour, cannons and balls — in the trophy in the centre of the picture.

Right (above): Looking across the cool marbled Great Hall to the doorway of the Saloon. The royal coat-of-arms on the arch and the other stone adornments are by Grinling Gibbons.

Right (below): Hawksmoor's ceiling in the Green Writing-Room.

gateway, copied from the back entrance to the public gardens at Vicenza.

If Sir William Chambers's improvements at Blenheim were generally on a restrained scale, Capability Brown pulled out all the stops. Whereas Vanbrugh's original designs had been treated with good manners by his architectural successor, Brown showed no such sympathy for Henry Wise's formal creations. The "military garden", or parterre, to the south, as well as the Great Court to the north, were simply grassed over. Even allowing for the possibility that the south garden had by the mid-1760s declined into less than immaculate order, it is surely impossible to forgive Brown for this particular act of ruthless vandalism carried out in accordance with the prevailing fashion for "nature". The historically-minded 9th Duke happily restored the formal arrangement of the Great Court but never achieved his ambition of putting back the parterre to the south and the area remains a vast, flat, featureless expanse of grass. In other respects Brown's achievement at Blenheim touched the sublime.

In 1764, the year he was commissioned by the 4th Duke of Marlborough to relandscape Blenheim, Brown, then in his late forties, was also appointed Surveyor to His Majesty's Gardens and Waters at Hampton Court. As a gardener at Stowe twenty-odd years previously, the young Northumbrian had been influenced by the landscape ideals of William Kent who, in Horace Walpole's words, "leaped the fence and saw that all nature was a garden". The "picturesque" approach was to bring the paintings of Claude and Poussin dramatically to life. Since leaving Stowe in 1749, Brown had been busy contriving serpentine lakes and clumps of trees so as to realize the "capabilities" of numerous gentlemens' estates – if not quite as numerous as some present-day owners would like to believe. In 1763 he was given a trial by the 4th Duke of Marlborough, producing a plan for the relandscaping of the family's secondary seat, Langley Park near Slough in Buckinghamshire, which his father had bought in 1738 from Lord Masham, widower of Duchess Sarah's detested cousin Abigail. "I like it very well," wrote the Duke from Blenheim in June, adding, "As I cannot begin to make alterations (at least *expensive* ones) at this place and at the same time, I have a notion I shall begin here immediately so that the sooner you come the better."

Brown found a landscape that must have seemed more than a little disconnected to his imaginative eye. There were some splendid features but somehow they did not form a coherent composition. The great seven-towered palace stood on a bare bank above a vast valley in which meandered the meagre River Glyme. Vanbrugh's Grand Bridge traversing the valley lacked the vital ingredient of something suitably aquatic underneath; the canal cobbled together out of the Glyme by the 1st Duke's military engineer, Colonel Armstrong, may have delighted his client, Duchess Sarah, but, to Horace Walpole, it "begged for a drop of water and was refused". In his *Plan for the Intended Alterations* (presumably prepared in the autumn of 1763), Brown proposed to give point to Vanbrugh's heroic bridge.

First, a hefty dam was built near Bladon, and then two causeways that had led from old Woodstock Manor across the meadows to the town of Woodstock and the city of Oxford respectively were cut through so as to enable the Glyme to gush through the bridge, spreading out into lakes on either side. As Dorothy Stroud, the authority on Capability Brown, has observed: "If these two lakes had been designed as one vast expanse of water, the effect would have been tedious. As it is they are both united yet divided by Vanbrugh's bridge from which the two parts spread out like the loops of a nicely tied bow." Duchess Sarah's old cascade (proudly described by her as "the finest and largest ever made") disappeared under water. Brown was no less proud of his own Grand Cascade at the western end of the lake; a noisy and dramatic exit for the water on its way to the River Evenlode by way of another, later cascade and Chambers's New Bridge.

The masterly creation excited Capability's contemporaries as much as it was to thrill subsequent generations. The 2nd Lord Cadogan, the brother of the 1st Duke of Marlborough's old comrade-in-arms, wrote to Brown: "The water is, by much, the finest artificial thing I ever saw; when I say that I include the banks and the advantageous manner in which you have set it off." Boswell remarked to Dr Johnson after touring the grounds: "You and I, Sir, have, I think, seen together the extremes of what

Overleaf (left): View down the Long Library towards the Willis organ. (Right): The Saloon which, with its murals and painted ceiling by Louis Laguerre "can vie with the most splendid palace rooms in Europe".

Below: Capability Brown's "Plan for the Intended alteration...", showing the Gothicizing of the buildings of Woodstock visible from the palace.

can be seen in Britain: the wild rough island of Mull, and Blenheim Park.'' Thomas Jefferson, the future American President, was particularly impressed by the cascade and noted that the park contained 2,500 acres, and that the turf required to be mown every ten days. As Sir Sacheverell Sitwell has summed it all up: the lake at Blenheim is ''the one great argument of the landscape-gardener. There is nothing finer in Europe.''

In censuring Capability Brown for his insensitivity to what had gone before in terms of formality, it would nevertheless be quite wrong to describe his ''picturesque'' approach as revolutionary with regard to Blenheim. Indeed it is striking, as both the supreme experts on the subject, David Green and Dorothy Stroud, have pointed out, how similar Brown's perception of the potentialities of the park was to the views expressed by Vanbrugh in his plea for preserving old Woodstock Manor. It was, after all, Vanbrugh himself who had observed:

> That Part of the Park which is Seen from the North front of the New Building, has Little Variety of Objects, Nor does the Country beyond it Afford any of Value. It therefore Stands in Need of all the help that can be given which are only Two: Buildings and plantations. These rightly dispos'd will indeed Supply all the Wants of Nature in the Place.

As for the plantations, Brown adorned the previously bare banks of the lakes with artistically proportioned groups of beech trees and small clumps of cedar of Lebanon and the recently-introduced Lombardy poplar. Elsewhere in the park, Brown planted an enclosing belt of beech trees, with ornamental species softening the effect on the inner edge. The high plateau to the north, the ''Great Park'', was made into two huge, unequal open spaces, one on either side of the original Grand Avenue, which Brown kept. These spaces were ornamented with great clumps to add to those already planted by Wise (thus a significant amount of his predecessor's landscaping was conserved). In the low-lying southern end of the park, the ''Lower Park'', more intimate, sheltered landscapes were arranged. The ancient and atmospheric oakwoods to the south-west were left intact without the beech fringe. All around the park, vistas were cunningly contrived through the enclosing shelter of beech so as to take in such features as the towers of Woodstock and Bladon churches.

The other ''Want of Nature'', buildings, also exercised Brown at Blenheim. Seeking ''eyecatchers'', he produced designs for Gothicizing the walls of the town of Woodstock that were visible from the park; for an elaborate gateway; and for an elaborate ''Bathing House'' at Rosamond's Well; but none of these projects was executed. Those that were, included the Gothic dressings on a granary and other outbuildings at Park Farm, the home farm in the Great Park to the north-west of the Column of Victory. He wrote to the Duke of Marlborough in 1765:

Opposite: More of Brown's Gothick schemes.
Above: The 1765 design for the granary at Park Farm.
Below: His plans (unexecuted) for a bathing house at Rosamund's Well.

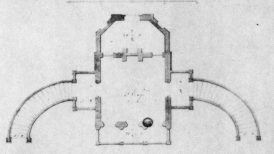
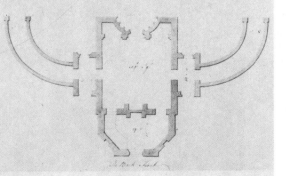

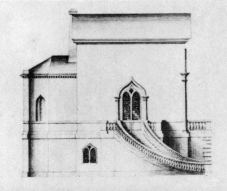
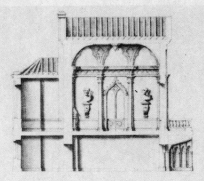

George DUKE of MARLBOROUGH—Caroline D.s of MARLBOROUGH—George MARQUISS of BLANDFORD—LORD Henry Spencer—LADY Caroline Spencer—LADY Eliz.t spencer—LADY Charlotte Spencer—LADY An.

PAINTED By Sir Joshua REYNO

Left: Sir Joshua Reynolds's group of the 4th Duke of Marlborough and his family which hangs in the Red Drawing-Room. The 1st Duke is represented by the statue in the right of the picture. The 4th Duke is shown in his Garter robes, holding one of the Marlborough Gems; while his youngest daughter, Lady Anne, is teased with a mask.

Above: Nathaniel Dance's faintly mischievous portrait of Lancelot (''Capability'') Brown, who transformed Blenheim's surroundings in the 1760s for the 4th Duke of Marlborough. ''I think I have made the River Thames blush today,'' Brown is said to have boasted after his lakes gave point to Vanbrugh's heroic bridge in the park.

I have enclosed to your Grace the Sketch for the Front of the cart House, Granery etc. I mean the Granery to have two Floors besides Stages for Corn between them for the easy turning of the Grain, and letting it fall from one floor to the other which is the best way of keeping it sweet; there may be very good convenience for Grain over the Cart Hovel if wanted, and upon a level with the Floor in the Square Granery. If a Barn is wanted, the middle part may be very eas[il]y made into one by taking a piece of the Cart House on one side, and piece of the supposed Stable on the other, and the arch will make a good Entrance or barn door. I have supposed a Habitation for a Family on the Corner next to the Column; some of the stone which has been pull'd down in the sunk fence, may if your Grace pleases be made use of for the front: and I flatter myself that the Effect of the Building would be very proper for the situation.

Brown was probably also responsible for the menagerie built near Park Farm where the 4th Duke of Marlborough was to emulate his royal predecessor, Henry I, in housing a tiger when one was sent to him in 1771 by Clive of India. And Brown very likely had a hand in the "antique battlements" applied to High Lodge. The oldest lodge at Blenheim, situated high up on the west side of the park, was once the residence of the Comptrollers, or Rangers, of Woodstock Park and Keeper of the King's Hawks. Its most famous, or notorious, occupant was the locally-born Restoration poet and libertine John Wilmot, 2nd Earl of Rochester, whom Charles II appointed to the sinecure. Rochester actually died here in 1680 ("The continual Course of Drinking and a perpetual Decay of his Spirits in Love and Writing had entirely broken his Constitution . . ."), having made his confession to his friend Bishop Burnet. The nineteenth-century American moralist Nathaniel Hawthorne, who considered Rochester's warm heart to be "faintly perceptible amid the dissolute trash which he left behind", mused that "if such good fortune ever befell a bookish man" he would choose this lodge for his "own residence with the topmost room of the tower for a study, and all the seclusion of cultivated wildness beneath to ramble in".

Brown transformed High Lodge, previously a plain two-storey house with dormers in a pitched roof that had been done up by Vanbrugh for the 1st Duke and Sarah for them to stay in during building operations at the palace, into a Gothic toy castle. Pointed windows were installed on both storeys of the principal front; a canted bay was added, rising to a higher level; and the old roof was disguised by a crenellated parapet. The lodge did not, in the event, become the retreat of a bookish man but a workaday estate tenement, also used for shooting lunches.

Capability Brown worked at Blenheim on and off for ten years between 1764 and 1774. His labours were fulsomely recorded by the Reverend William Mavor, Rector of Woodstock and tutor to Lord Blandford, in his *New Description of Blenheim* (1787):

> In this singularly picturesque landscape, the beautiful and the sublime are most intimately combined: all that can please, elevate, or astonish, display themselves at once . . . No awkward termination is here to be traced; no disgusting display of art to heighten the scene . . . The Park . . . is one continued galaxy of charming prospects, agreeably diversified scenes. Its circumference is upwards of twelve miles; its area about two thousand seven hundred acres, round which are the most enchanting rides, chiefly shaded towards the boundary with a deep belt of various trees, evergreens, and deciduous shrubs, whose mingled foliage exhibit the different gradations of tints from the most faint to the most obfuscated green.

A more technical record was drawn up in 1789 by Thomas Pride and his invaluable survey of the park was incorporated into subsequent editions of the Rector's paean. The faithful Mr Mavor was liable to break into verse at every opportunity to celebrate the greater glory of Blenheim, penning odes, for instance, "On Launching the *Sovereign*, a Magnificent Pleasure-Boat on the Lake at Blenheim" and "On Converting the Green-House into a Private Theatre". Although long on purple description and short on hard fact, Mavor's *New Description of Blenheim* (which ran to thirteen editions, the last being published in 1846) gives a delightful picture of the palace in its late-Georgian heyday; an annotated reprint would surely make a welcome addition to the Blenheim bibliography.

The salient hard fact at the time Mavor sung the praises of Blenheim was the expense of it all. As the 2nd Lord Cadogan observed, there was a danger of the 4th Duke of Marlborough's embellishments literally beggaring description. Capability Brown received over £21,500 for work in hand during his ten-year stint in the park. Here, as Thomas Jefferson noted in his *Memorandum*, 200 people were employed in its upkeep and 2,000 fallow deer and 2,500 sheep roamed.

But the crippling element in country house economics is not so much the capital expenditure on improvements – though obviously they can have a decisive effect – as the drip-drip-drip of the maintenance costs. In the 4th Duke's time some 187 rooms at the palace (not counting "many other Rooms in the South East and other of the Towers") were furnished and in use. In a "Memorandum for her Grace", the Duchess was informed that there were 30 rooms on the principal floor (in addition to the Hall, Saloon and Library), 40 rooms on the bedroom floor, 15 rooms on the mezzanine in between (for the upper servants), 20 rooms in the basement, plus 12 on Bachelor's Row, 14 in the "Heights", 28 in the Arcade and Court Yard and 17 in the stables.

Left: Aerial view of the park, with the two lakes divided by Vanbrugh's Grand Bridge in the centre. Woodstock is to the left, Bladon beyond the palace in the upper left of the picture. Note the landscaping of the trees and Brown's clumps.

Top: Sir William Chambers's pleasing New Bridge across the River Glyme at the Bladon end of the park.

Above: High Lodge in its lush setting on the edge of the park.

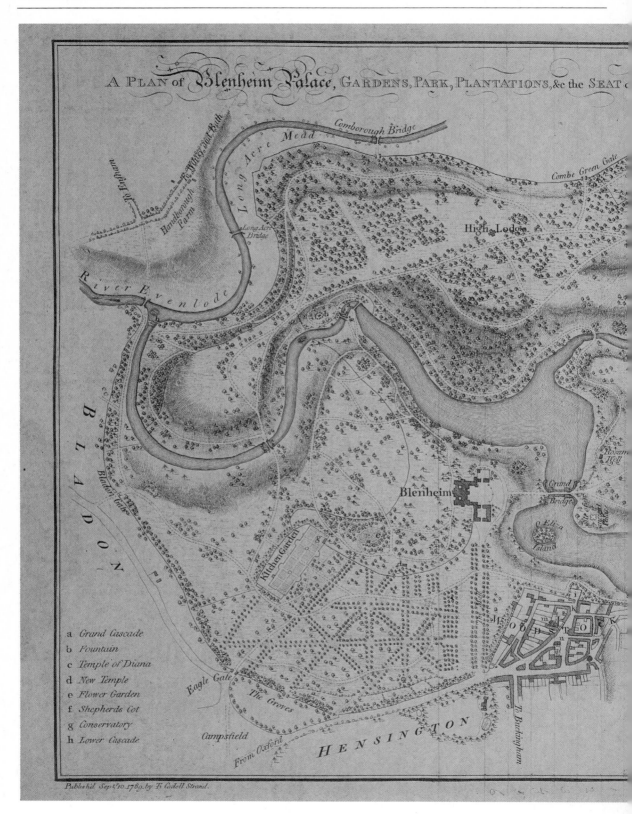

A PLAN of Blenheim Palace, GARDENS, PARK, PLANTATIONS, &c the SEAT

a Grand Cascade
b Fountain
c Temple of Diana
d New Temple
e Flower Garden
f Shepherds Cot
g Conservatory
h Lower Cascade

Survey of the park by Thomas Pride, 1789, which was incorporated in Mavor's New Description of Blenheim.

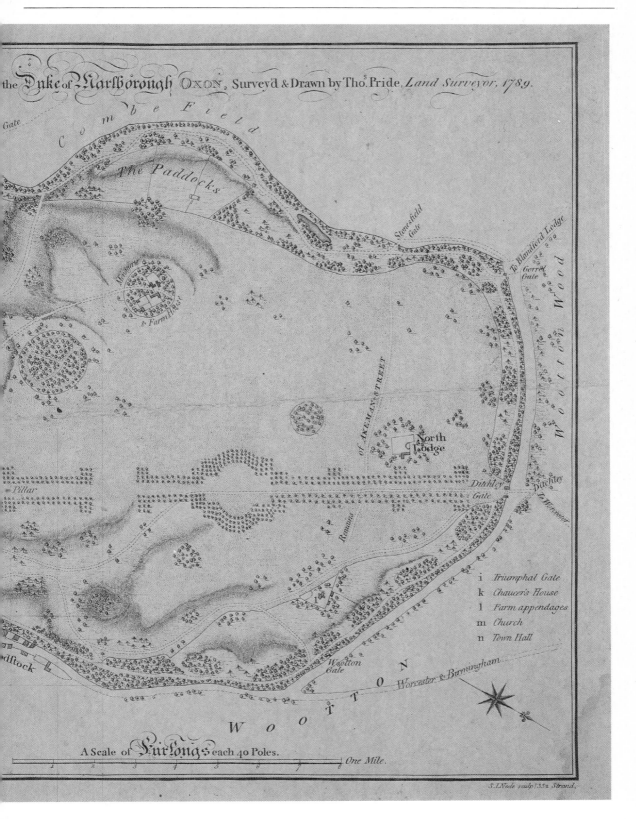

the Duke of Marlborough, Oxon, Surveyd & Drawn by Thos. Pride, Land Surveyor, 1789.

Gate

Combe Field

The Paddocks

Stonesfield Gate

To Blandford Lodge

Garret Gate

Woodstock

& Farm House

North Lodge

OF AKEMANS STREET

Pillar

Remains

Ditchley Gate

Ditchley

To Worcester

i   Triumphal Gate
k   Chaucer's House
l   Farm appendages
m   Church
n   Town Hall

Woolton Gate

Worcester & Birmingham

W O O T T O N

A Scale of Furlongs each 40 Poles.

One Mile.

S. J. Neele sculp 352 Strand.

George, 5th Duke of Marlborough: botanist, bibliophile and (virtual) bankrupt.

George, 6th Duke of Marlborough: sportsman and suspected bigamist.

The wage bill for the Blenheim household staff of 75 (previously 87) at that time came to a seemingly modest £785 9s. 2¾d. Those on the pay-roll included a running footman, who on a diet of white wine and eggs, could maintain a steady pace of some seven miles per hour beside the ducal carriage. In the eighteenth century it was regarded as a jolly diversion – also, of course, a useful betting medium – for the running footman to race against his master's horse and carriage. In her *Notebooks* the Victorian anecdotist Lady Dorothy Nevill tells the story of the last such race on record between the 4th Duke of Marlborough (in a carriage and four) and his footman from Windsor to London. The running footman just failed to overhaul the Duke and died from the effects of overstrain.

Labour, even life, may have been comparatively cheap but the bills were beginning to pile up. Apart from the expense of improving and maintaining Blenheim, there was Marlborough House in London (where Sir William Chambers did some remodelling), Langley Park in Buckinghamshire and the newly acquired Cornbury (later the seat of the Watney brewers) in Wychwood Forest near Blenheim, not to mention the price to be paid for transporting the whole caravan from cooks to laundrymaids around the country. Cuts would have to be made. Langley was sold in 1788; Marlborough House, which had only been leased by Sarah, was to revert to the Crown on the 4th Duke's death in 1817, half-a-dozen miserable years after his Duchess.

As his long reign at Blenheim wore on, the 4th Duke became less and less sociable. Visitors were not welcome, however distinguished. In the summer of 1802 Nelson, the victor of the Nile, turned up at Blenheim with his mistress Emma Hamilton and her complaisant elderly husband Sir William, but the 4th Duke did not feel up to receiving such a party and eventually had some refreshments sent out to them in the park. This did not go down well and the provender was promptly returned. The flamboyant Emma declared that if Marlborough's services had been rewarded with Blenheim it was because a woman had then reigned, "and women have great souls". She said that if she herself were Queen, Nelson would already have received a principality that would make Blenheim seem like a kitchen garden – a remark which moved the great Admiral to tears. The imagination boggles at what Emma would have expected Nelson to receive after Trafalgar three years later, if he had not been killed. (In the event, Nelson's descendants have certainly suffered in comparison with the Spencer-Churchills, the late Earl Nelson being a landless publican, and his nephew, the present Earl, being a Detective Sergeant in Welwyn Garden City.)

"The Duke had been for some time a confirmed hypochondriac," recalled the Society buck, Gronow, in his *Reminiscences*, "and dreaded anything that could in any way ruffle the tranquil monotony of his existence." Gronow continued,

It is said that he remained for three years without pronouncing a single word, and was entering the fourth year of his silence when he was told one morning that Madame la Baronne de Staël, the authoress of *Corinne*, was on the point of arriving to pay him a visit. The Duke immediately recovered his speech and roared out, "Take me away – take me away!" to the utter astonishment of the circle around him, who all declared that nothing but the terror of this literary visitation could have put an end to this long and obstinate monomania.

The gossipy Gronow also claimed that the 4th Duke's heir, Lord Blandford, had once shown him £50,000 in notes, all of which the feckless young man had borrowed. "You see Gronow," said Lord Blandford, "how the immense fortune of my family will be frittered away; but I can't help it, I must live. My father inherited £50,000 in ready money and £70,000 a year in land; and in all probability when it comes to my turn to live at Blenheim I shall have nothing left but the annuity of £5,000 a year on the Post Office."

It was just as well that the family estates were entailed, otherwise Blenheim's continuity of ownership could easily have come a cropper during the twenty-three-year reign of George, the profligate 5th Duke of Marlborough, who succeeded his father after the 4th Duke died "suddenly" at Blenheim in January 1817. Born in 1766 and educated at Eton and Christ Church, Oxford, he sat in the House of Commons as a Tory for Oxfordshire and late insouciantly changing sides, as a Whig for Tregeny in Cornwall, but made little impact on public life. He earns a footnote in studies of the peerage for being, as Lord Blandford, the first nobleman to style himself "Marquess" in the now accepted English manner instead of using the foreign "Marquis". In 1791 he married Lady Susan Stewart, daughter of the 7th Earl of Galloway and they set up home at White Knights, near Reading, where he lashed out enormous sums on his beloved collections of books and plants.

For all his reckless extravagance, the Marquess was a scholar and a man of taste. His purchase in 1812 of Boccaccio's *Decameron* (printed by Valdarfer in 1471) for £2,260, at the dispersal of the famous library of the Duke of Roxburghe, led to the formation of the Roxburghe Club, a convivial gathering of bibliophiles with himself to the fore. His wife Susan shared his love of botany, producing some exceptionally fine watercolours of flowers (preserved in the Long Library), but they spent much of the time apart. In addition to his four sons and a daughter by Susan, Blandford also had an illegitimate daughter by his mistress, Lady Mary Anne Sturt, wife of the squire of Crichel in Dorset. The affair ended acrimoniously with an action for adultery in 1801 when, for once, the free-spending heir to Blenheim got off lightly, having to find only £100 of the £20,000 damages claimed.

Above: The room (formerly one of the apartments occupied by Dean Jones, the 1st Duke's Chaplain) where Sir Winston Churchill was born on 30 November 1874. To the left of the picture are Sir Winston's maroon velvet boiler-suit, which he found restful to wear during his round-the-clock watches in the Second World War, and his monogrammed slippers.

Left: A cutting of Sir Winston's curls, taken when he was aged five, which are on display in the same room.

The Budget *by Sir Max Beerbohm, 1910. The original of this celebrated cartoon is also on show in Sir Winston Churchill's Birth Room in the palace. Churchill is reassuring his clearly alarmed cousin, Sunny, 9th Duke of Marlborough: "Come, come, as I said in one of my speeches, 'There is nothing in the budget to make it harder for a poor hardworking man to keep a small home in decent comfort.'" The "small home" in the background is, of course, Blenheim Palace.*

When he eventually succeeded to Blenheim in 1817, the 5th Duke of Marlborough took the additional surname of Churchill by Royal Licence. His father and grandfather's surname had been simply "Spencer" but he (and, of course, all his descendants) became "Spencer-Churchill". Possibly the recent Battle of Waterloo may have had some influence on his decision; the family doubtless wanted to remind people of earlier military glories associated with the illustrious name of Churchill.

The beginning of his reign at Blenheim was marked by a magnificently arranged celebration. The orders of the day were:

The stable people to be stationed on the steps when the company arrive . . . The lamps round the court, steps and portico to be lighted by nine . . . The other servants to be ranged in the Hall to announce the company and conduct them through the Bow Window Room to the Grand Cabinet. The double doors to be opened as far as the Dining Room . . . The band to play in the Hall while the company arrive, then in the Dining Room as they pass to the Saloon. They will afterwards return to the Hall and during dessert play at the door leading to the Saloon. When the ladies retire they will cease and be ready to recommence in the Library when the gentlemen go to the Drawing Room. A person will attend to give them refreshments in the Colonnade, but *on no account whatever* must anything be taken into the Library.

In the twelfth edition of his guide book to Blenheim Mavor describes how the 5th Duke did up the rooms underneath the Long Library (now the restaurant and cafeteria) with:

Waterloo blue puckered drapery, ornamented at intervals with black rosettes, and a large rosette of the same material in the centre of the ceiling, from which all the ribs of the drapery diverge. This room looks immediately on to the Arcade Flower Garden and a pavilion of an octagon form composed of various coloured woods with their natural bark. This is supported by columns of yew with a carved colonnade around it. Two other apartments are now added, the one a Withdrawing Room fitted up entirely with a Japan wainscoting round a painted representation of a Tiger Hunt in India . . . The Refectory is in imitation of an Italian Dining Room of Verd d'Antique and Sienna marble, with corresponding columns and doorcases. The doors are of polished Blenheim oak and the floors tessellated with oak and with acacia also grown in Blenheim Park.

Out in the grounds, down towards the Grand Cascade, the 5th Duke determined to create "the finest botanical and flower garden in England". Mavor's guide relies on the description of the botanist Dr Bowles; we learn of New Holland or Botany Bay Garden, the Chinese Garden and the Dahlia Garden, "all surrounded with borders of seedling oaks, kept constantly cut"; the

Swiss Cottage, "the residence of the watchman to the Private Gardens, in viewing which the mind is carried back to the early delights of reading the story of Robinson Crusoe and his village of bark". Dr Bowles's passages on the Druid's Temple ("an altar formed by an immense tablet of rock and supported by huge pillars of unhewn stone, overgrown with moss"), a Trysting Tree, the Valley of Streams, a Garden of Springs, the Shepherd's Cot, grottoes and other rustic fantasies conjure up a veritable horticultural cornucopia. The visitor, he suggested, would experience "a feeling of deliciously complete delight, a dreamy deliquium of the soul, which 'brings down hours to moments' and steeps the senses in luxurious forgetfulness".

It was, of course, all too good to last. The 5th Duke's wallow in luxurious forgetfulness was brusquely disturbed by the arrival of bailiffs at Blenheim. As the principal heirlooms were happily protected by entail, White Knights and his own library had to be sold to meet some of his debts. The bibliophile Duke made a thumping loss on his books (4,701 lots going for less than £14,500); the Boccaccio was picked up by his cousin, the 2nd Earl Spencer, President of the Roxburghe Club, for only 875 guineas, well under half what the spendthrift Spencer-Churchill had paid for it. The Duke's desperate attempts to raise some cash earned him the reputation with the acid Mrs Arbuthnot of being a common swindler.

Retrenchment inevitably became the order of the day. And so Blenheim entered the Victorian age in a distinctly run-down condition. During the latter years of the 5th Duke, as the *Annual Register* for 1840 (the year of his death) remarked, "he lived in utter retirement at one corner of his magnificent palace, a melancholy instance of the results of extravagance."

The 5th Duke's eldest son and heir, yet another George, left little mark at Blenheim during his reign which lasted from 1840 to 1857, save for some rather endearingly rude marginalia in his annotated copy of the last edition of Mavor's guide book to the palace. Next to the platitude "when men begin to reason they cease to feel", the 6th Duke of Marlborough scrawled "Nonsense". Reason does not seem to have been a strong point of the young heir. At Eton he was the principal ring-leader in the "Keate riots" when the boys violently rebelled against their notoriously disciplinarian, if diminutive, Headmaster. One of the 6th Duke's schoolfellows, Lord Monson, described him as "one of the handsomest lads I ever saw"; the combination of good looks and great expectations proved irresistible to women, particularly to a Miss Susan Law by whom he had an illegitimate daughter. In a subsequent libel case, heard in 1838, it was alleged that Lord Blandford had seduced the innocent young girl from a respectable family by means of a mock marriage. The farcical ceremony, performed by his army officer brother in the guise of a clergyman under the eyes of Miss Law's mother at her home in

Bryanston Square, supposedly took place in 1817, but had not come to light until many years later when the *Satirist* gossip sheet claimed Lord Blandford's marriage to his cousin Lady Jane Stewart (daughter of his mother's brother, the 8th Earl of Galloway) was bigamous. Although some honour for the good name of the Marlboroughs was salvaged when it was revealed that Lord Blandford's mother had been paying £400 a year to Miss Law (later halved), the judge delivered himself of some judicious remarks about Lord Blandford's moral character.

After the death of Lady Jane in 1744, the 6th Duke of Marlborough, an energetic all-round sportsman until his health gave way and he was confined to a wheelchair, married twice more. His second wife, Charlotte Flower, daughter of the 4th Viscount Ashbrook, lived for less than four years after the wedding, but the third wife, another Stewart cousin (also called Jane), was to survive him by nearly forty years, dying in 1897. There were three sons (the eldest was called, for a change, John, after the 1st Duke) and a daughter (who married a Spencer cousin) by the first marriage; another son and daughter by the second; and a fifth son by the third.

Towards the end of his largely unrecorded reign at Blenheim, the 6th Duke became entangled in an extraordinary public debate over the admission price for visitors to Blenheim which was conducted in the correspondence columns of the *Illustrated London News* and *The Times*. In reply to complaints, a spokesman for the palace pointed out that while the maximum charge was admittedly five shillings, for three days a week no ticket was required ("a privilege which is a great tax upon the Marlborough family"). The anonymous protagonist then patronizingly urged the Duke to show the same faith as those

> noblemen who zealously endeavour to elevate the tastes of the humbler classes by lectures, by libraries, by social gatherings, inviting them to visit their domains and encouraging their rustic sports; weaning them from the brawls of the beershop and making them enjoy, in the company of their wives, their families and their neighbours, social intercourse and innocent recreation in the open air . . .

Shortly before he died in 1857, the 6th Duke duly cut the cost of a ticket to visit Blenheim down to one shilling.

The 7th Duke of Marlborough had been the sitting member for Woodstock in the House of Commons until his father's death. An earnest, plodding and rather dreary figure (nicely described by A.L. Rowse as "a complete full-blown Victorian prig"), he had distinguished himself in politics as the author of the doubtless worthy "Blandford Act", in the year before his father died, which enabled the sub-division of extensive parishes. In 1866 he became a Privy Councillor and Lord Steward of the Household; the following year Lord President of the Council and later

Opposite: John, 7th Duke of Marlborough, "a complete full-blown Victorian prig".

Viceroy of Ireland where as the *Dictionary of National Biography* somewhat flatly records "His administration was . . . popular, and he endeavoured to benefit the trade of the country." His Vicereine, the formidable Duchess Fanny, daughter of the erratic 3rd Marquess of Londonderry, endeared herself to the Irish by her energetic fund-raising for famine relief when the potato crop failed again during their four-year stint at Viceregal Lodge in Dublin. She was inordinately proud of a personal letter from Queen Victoria thanking her for her efforts; she had a tendency to brandish this royal epistle with the admonition: "You realize that in my life, I have been of some use to my fellow subjects."

Duchess Fanny produced eleven children, five sons and six girls, but only two of the sons survived childhood; in the event, she was to outlive both of these strange and unhappy characters, George (briefly the 8th Duke) and her favourite, Randolph. George, who was expelled from Eton and became a notorious lecher, married Lady Albertha Hamilton, one of the seven daughters of the 1st Duke of Abercorn who all married peers. "Goosie", as her sobriquet implies, was rather a wearisome girl with a distressing penchant for practical jokes (apple-pie beds, knotted pyjamas, inkpots over the door and, on one notorious

Opposite: The wife of the 7th Duke of Marlborough, the formidable Duchess Fanny.
Above (left): Her younger son, the future politician Lord Randolph Churchill.
Above (right): Her daughter-in-law, Lady Albertha ("Goosie") Hamilton, who married her elder son, George, Marquess of Blandford (later 8th Duke of Marlborough).

occasion, a celluloid baby doll concealed under a breakfast egg cover) that drove Blandford, very far from an ideal husband, to distraction. Randolph, who was to have a meteoric political career, married Jennie Jerome, a spirited American girl he had met at Cowes and proposed to almost immediately.

In *The Reminiscences of Lady Randolph Churchill* (1908) Jennie Jerome recalled her first impressions of Blenheim:

> My first visit to Blenheim was on a beautiful spring day in May, 1874. Some of the Duke's tenants and Randolph's constituents met us at the station to give us a welcome, and taking the horses out of the carriage, insisted on dragging us through the town to the house. The place could not have looked more glorious, and as we passed through the entrance archway, and the lovely scenery burst upon me, Randolph said with pardonable pride, "This is the finest view in England." Looking at the lake, the bridge, the miles of magnificent park studded with old oaks, I found no adequate words to express my admiration, and when we reached the huge and stately palace, where I was to find hospitality for so many years, I confess that I felt awed. But my American pride forbade the admission.

Jennie Churchill also noted the "most dignified, and indeed, somewhat formal style" in which her parents-in-law lived:

> At luncheon, rows of entrée dishes adorned the table, joints beneath massive silver covers being placed before the Duke and Duchess, who each carved for the whole company, and as this included governesses, tutors, and children, it was no sinecure.
>
> Before leaving the dining-room, the children filled with food small baskets kept for the purpose for poor cottagers or any who might be sick or sorry in Woodstock. These they distributed in the course of their afternoon walks.
>
> When the house was full for a shooting-party, even breakfast was made a ceremonious meal, and no one dreamed of beginning until all had assembled. The ladies would be dressed in long velvet or silk trains . . .
>
> When the family were alone at Blenheim, everything went on with the regularity of clockwork. So assiduously did I practise my piano, read, or paint, that I began to imagine myself back in the school-room. In the morning an hour or more was devoted to the reading of newspapers, which was a necessity, if one wanted to show an intelligent interest in the questions of the day, for at dinner conversation invariably turned on politics. In the afternoon a drive to pay a visit to some neighbor, or a walk in the gardens, would help to while away some part of the day. After dinner, which was a rather solemn full-dress affair, we all repaired to what was called the Vandyke [sic] room. There one might read one's book, or play

Lady Randolph Churchill, the former Jennie Jerome, Sir Winston Churchill's American mother.

Opposite: The 7th Duke of Marlborough and his family outside the east front of the palace.

for love a mild game of whist. Many a glance would be cast at the clock, which sometimes would be surreptitiously advanced a quarter of an hour by some sleepy member of the family. No one dared suggest bed until the sacred hour of eleven had struck. Then we would all troop out into a small anteroom, and lighting our candles, each in turn would kiss the Duke and Duchess and depart to our own rooms.

After some polite remarks about the kindness and old-world courtesy of the Duke and the intelligence and warm-heartedness of the Duchess, Jennie reveals something of her true feelings about her mother-in-law: "She ruled Blenheim and nearly all those in it with a firm hand. At the rustle of her silk dress the household trembled."

In fairness to Duchess Fanny it could be said that she was obliged to run the palace on a tight rein for reasons of economy. The Marlboroughs' income of £40,000 a year was by no means great by contemporary ducal standards, certainly not with Blenheim to maintain. Rather than retreat to a corner like the spent-out 5th Duke, they managed to keep up appearances, dutifully entertaining the Prince of Wales and other notables of the day – even if sometimes the fare was somewhat sparse. Sir Alexander Cockburn, the Lord Chief Justice, complained in the Visitors' Book that while he was prepared to share almost everything in life, he drew the line at half a snipe for dinner.

It was while out with the guns during a shooting party at Blenheim in November 1874 that the pregnant Jennie had a fall. This, followed a few days later by what her husband described as "a rather imprudent and rough drive in a pony carriage" prematurely brought on Jennie's labour pains. For the delivery she was installed in an unprepossessing small bedroom in the former apartments of Dean Jones, the 1st Duke's rotund chaplain, just off the Great Hall.

The 7th Duke's chaplain duly christened the baby that was safely born, after eight hours' labour, "Winston Leonard "in the palace Chapel. (The first half of the surname Spencer-Churchill was later quietly dropped by the historically-minded heir presumptive to the dukedom of Marlborough.) Today "Sir Winston Churchill's Birth Room", with the Churchill Exhibition nearby, is one of the main attractions for visitors to Blenheim. Among the items on show in the bedroom are the young Winston's red curls, the maroon velvet boiler suit he found it comfortable to wear during the Second World War and the original of Sir Max Beerbohm's celebrated cartoon of 1910, "The Budget". "Come, come as I said in one of my speeches," Winston is reassuring his cousin, the 9th Duke of Marlborough, "There is nothing in the budget to make it harder for a poor hardworking man to keep a small home in decent comfort." In the background Max has drawn an outline of Blenheim.

For Winston's grandfather, the 7th Duke, however, money worries were no laughing matter. To stave off another catastrophe of the sort his own grandfather had precipitated, the upright Victorian statesman sold the Marlborough Gems, in one lot at Christie's, in 1875. The sparkling collection of jewels and cameos, so cherished by his great-grandfather, the 4th Duke, went for £10,000. Much worse was to come, though for the moment matters of morality meant more to the Marlboroughs than money.

Tired of his wife's practical jokes, the bounderish Lord Blandford had sought comfort elsewhere and found it with the devil-may-care wife of the Earl of Aylesford, the former Edith Williams. In February 1876 Edith wrote to "Sporting Joe" Aylesford – then out in India, where he was shooting tigers – informing her husband that she and Lord Blandford intended to elope. Such behaviour was scandalous enough in Victorian times, but what turned the Aylesford Affair into a sensation was the involvement of Albert Edward, the Prince of Wales, who was himself a former admirer of Edith's and a racing crony of her husband. All the participants in the saga were part of the Prince's "Marlborough House Set" (so named after the royal residence that had, of course, once been the London home of the Dukes of Marlborough) and it was the Prince who had taken Sporting Joe to India.

The delicate situation was aggravated by the impulsive intervention of Lord Randolph Churchill who went to astonishing extremes in his attempts to prevent what he called "a fearful family disaster". After failing to persuade his royal friend to intervene, Lord Randolph accused the Prince of Wales of being responsible for the whole business by having arranged for Sporting Joe to come to India in the first place. When this had little effect, other than infuriating the Prince, Lord Randolph, with Edith Aylesford in tow, went round to Marlborough House where he threatened the Princess of Wales that he was "aware of peculiar and most grave matters affecting the case". The excitable Lord Randolph finally spelt it out in an interview with the royal intermediary, Lord Hardwicke, who reported back to the Prince in India "that having letters to prove Your Royal Highness's own admiration for Lady Aylesford, they would prevent any divorce by using this powerful lever in any way they might think fit". In short, Lord Randolph was prepared to blackmail the heir to the throne in order to save the reputation of the Spencer-Churchills.

Far from being saved, of course, the family's reputation sank dramatically. In the summer of 1876 the Prince of Wales let it be known that neither he nor the Princess would accept invitations to houses where the Churchills were received. The Prime Minister, Disraeli (who had observed "Blandford, I always thought was a scoundrel but this brother beats him"), tactfully persuaded the 7th Duke of Marlborough to accept the post of Viceroy of Ireland in succession to Goosie Blandford's father, the Duke of Abercorn. "Blenheim," wrote Sir Winston Churchill in his biography of his father, "was handed over to housekeepers and agents and its household bodily transported to the Viceregal Lodge."

The banishment of the Spencer-Churchills proved only temporary and by the mid-1880s the Prince of Wales was fully reconciled with Lord Randolph. As things turned out, Sporting Joe Aylesford, a less than convincing innocent party, did not divorce Edith, emigrated to Texas and died of drink in 1885. Edith and Blandford's affair carried on until about the same time.

Unpublished letters from Blandford to Edith (whom he called "Toby") reveal rather affecting vignettes of their relationship: drives in hansom cabs through the gas-lit streets of London, trysts at Boulogne, Bournemouth and the unlikely romantic setting of Maidenhead Railway Station. Often Blandford wrote twice a day, larding the letters with lively gossip (the Prince of Wales always being referred to as "the monster"). But the seeds of future trouble between them already existed for while the liberated Edith did not care a fig for being ostracized by "Society", Blandford deeply minded the cuts.

Nonetheless, the outcast lovers set up house together as "Mr and Mrs Spencer" in Paris where a bastard son, registered as "Guy Bertrand", was born in 1881. Two years later (in the same year that Goosie Blandford finally divorced her husband, on the obvious grounds, shortly before he succeeded to the dukedom of Marlborough) young Guy, by now optimistically styled "Lord Guernsey" as if he were the son and heir of the Earl of Aylesford, was baptized at St Mary-le-Strand in London. When Sporting Joe died, however, the House of Lords disallowed such a paternity claim. For his true parents the painful case effectively put paid to their love affair. The new Duke of Marlborough was obliged to give evidence at the hearing and shortly afterwards parted from Edith – though he actually pleaded with her to let him bring up young Guy, whom he said he loved better than any of his four children (one son and three daughters) by Goosie.

At the time Edith was abandoned by the 8th Duke she was living, in comparative poverty, at "The Chalet", Farnham. When she died, in 1897, the Prince and Princess of Wales sent a wreath to the funeral. The epilogue to the Aylesford saga, however, cannot be satisfactorily concluded as so little is known of what became of Guy. Apparently known as "Bill Spencer", he was last seen by a member of the Churchill family walking alone in Chelsea some time after the Second World War.

Upon his return to Blenheim in 1880 from Viceregal Lodge, Dublin, the 7th Duke of Marlborough's money worries seemed more pressing than ever. With the appalling perspicacity of which only a high-minded prig could have been capable, he devised a scheme whereby the entail could be broken by an Act of Parliament. Thanks to the Blenheim Settled Estates Act of the same year (pushed through by the Duke's friend Earl Cairns, the Lord Chancellor), the Marlborough heirlooms lost their protected status. At the end of 1881 the first lots of the fabulous Sunderland Library went on sale; by the time the auctioning was completed in the summer of 1882 the 18,000 volumes had fetched nearly £60,000. Then, coolly collecting a grant of £2,000 for the purpose, the 7th Duke converted the Library ("whose beautiful old leather bindings," in Jennie Churchill's words, "decorated as nothing else can the immense long gallery with its white, carved book-cased and vaulted ceiling") into a picture gallery – doubtless justifying himself by pointing out that that was Vanbrugh's idea for the great room anyway.

Soon few great pictures, apart from family portraits, would be left in the palace to hang in such a gallery. The 8th Duke of Marlborough wanted some cash to modernize the farms, to put up some orchid houses (though their exotic blooms had to be sold themselves later), and to install electricity and a pioneering private telephone system, to convert some of the bedrooms into laboratories for his chemical and electrical experiments. To the 8th Duke, a technical genius who is said to have anticipated at least one of Edison's inventions, science came before art.

Works by Rembrandt, Rubens, Titian and numerous other celebrated artists duly disappeared from the walls of Blenheim up to Christie's in London for dispersal. Raphael's *Ansidei Madonna* (sold for £70,000), formerly in the Green Drawing-Room, and Van Dyck's famous equestrian *Charles I* (£17,500), which had dominated the northern end of the Library, both went to the National Gallery. Hundreds of other heirlooms also came under the hammer.

Nobody was angrier about this appalling philistinism than the Duke's brother Lord Randolph Churchill, but his protests were to no avail. Lord Randolph had entered Parliament as a Tory in 1874 and became leader of the so-called "Fourth Party" that made life difficult for his own front bench in the early 1880s. He revived and rejoiced in the appellation "Tory Radical", pressing for a more democratic set-up in the Conservative Party and vigorously opposing defence expenditure. Having achieved the Chancellorship of the Exchequer at the age of thirty-seven, he made the fatal mistake of resigning a few months later. He thought he was indispensable; when he learnt of his successor, he said "I forgot Goschen." Lord Randolph has gone down in history as a brilliant failure.

Notwithstanding his differences with his equally erratic brother, Lord Randolph could be said to have been indirectly instrumental in finding him a new bride. On a visit to America, in 1888, the 8th Duke met an acquaintance of the Jeromes (Lord Randolph's in-laws), Lily Hammersley, a rich widow, whom he

Lily, the American second wife of the 8th Duke of Marlborough, who gave Blenheim its boathouse and organ. She dropped her baptismal "Lilian" to avoid the inevitable rhyme with "million".

The erratic and brilliant Spencer-Churchill brothers. Above: The 8th Duke of Marlborough, some of whose scientific experiments anticipated Edison.

Right: Lord Randolph, the meteoric politician who resigned too hastily ("I forgot Goschen . . .") and died of syphilis.

The boathouse in about 1900 (top) and more recently (below). It was built in 1888 of stone with Gothic mullions and surmounted by a half-timbered chalet.

The inscription reads: "SO MAY THY CRAFT GLIDE GENTLY ON AS YEARS ROLL DOWN THE STREAM".

promptly married at New York City Hall. "There is no doubt," noted Jennie's colourful father Leonard Jerome, "that she has lots of tin."

Duchess Lily (the baptismal "Lilian" was dropped for fear of lampoons playing on the rhyme with "million") obligingly spent a fair amount of her tin on such items at Blenheim as releading the roof and installing central heating. The most notable legacies from her four years as *châtelaine* are the mighty Willis organ and the boathouse. The organ was installed in 1891 at the southern end of the Library (later moved to the northern end, where the equestrian Van Dyck had once been) and given a rousing send-off by the composer Sir Arthur Sullivan and others including the organist of Westminster Abbey. The inscription – "IN MEMORY OF HAPPY DAYS & AS A TRIBUTE TO THIS GLORIOUS HOME WE LEAVE THY VOICE TO SPEAK WITHIN THESE WALLS IN YEARS TO COME WHEN OURS ARE STILL" – was taken from a scrap of paper found among the 8th Duke's things after his death. The inscriptions on the boathouse read: "BUILT BY GEORGE CHARLES AND LILY WARREN DUKE AND DUCHESS OF MARLBOROUGH ANNO 1888" and, facing the lake, "SO MAY THY CRAFT GLIDE GENTLY ON AS YEARS ROLL DOWN THE STREAM".

The 8th Duke of Marlborough is remembered as the "Wicked Duke". After his death there were supposed to be disagreeable psychical manifestations in the rooms at Blenheim that he had used as laboratories. On hearing that these rooms had a bad reputation, one guest insisted on spending the night in one of them. The next morning he reported his hideous ordeal. "I was in bed with a corpse," he said, "and it was giving me electric shocks."

None the less, the 8th Duke had a considerable potential that was realized even less than his equally erratic brother's. "I have known one or two first-class minds whose achievements have been nil," wrote Moreton Frewen who was married to Jennie Churchill's sister. "Take George, eighth Duke of Marlborough, an almost incomparable mind, indeed in receptivity, range and versatility, hardly to be matched . . ." Lord Redesdale, grandfather to the Mitford sisterhood, recalled in his *Memoirs* that Duke George was "a youth of great promise marred by fate, shining in many branches of human endeavour, clever, capable of great industry, and within measurable distances of reaching conspicuous success in science, mathematics and mechanics."

The 8th Duke of Marlborough died "somewhat suddenly" at Blenheim in November 1892, aged forty-eight, predeceasing his younger brother, Lord Randolph (who died a terrible death of syphilis), by less than three years.

Blenheim's internal telephone system was installed in the 1880s by the 8th Duke of Marlborough, a mechanical genius.

5. Sunny

For the reign at Blenheim of the 9th Duke of Marlborough we can reach back within living memory. His grandson, the present Duke, was a boy of eight when the 9th Duke died in 1934. Among the Blenheim stalwarts still living in retirement about the place who can recall the days of the 9th Duke are the old woodman Harry Stockford, the plumber Sid Jakeman (whose father stoked the boilers at Blenheim for sixty-seven years), Phon Hollis and his nephew Bill, whose service dynasty kept the Woodstock Lodge gate and worked in the gardens. Their memories of the diminutive 9th Duke (looking "like a little boy") include seeing him riding around the park (he was a dapper horseman), planting hundreds of trees, supervising the construction of the water terraces, and celebrating his sixtieth birthday in spectacular style with a torchlight procession up to a bonfire by the Column of Victory. (In fact, an inadvertent miscalculation was made for the 9th Duke was only fifty-nine at the time.)

The 9th Duke's sobriquet of "Sunny" derived from his early days as Earl of Sunderland and proved anything but appropriate to his melancholy, unhappy disposition. However, his Aunt Maud, the Marchioness of Lansdowne, recalled that up to the age of ten he was one of the most charming boys she ever met, "& most joyous; after that his spirits seemed to have vanished". The reason is not hard to find. "He was wounded as a child," his second wife Gladys told her biographer Hugo Vickers and on top of the damage done by his parents' messy divorce in the wake of the Aylesford scandal, Sunny was bullied by his father. He was still up at Cambridge, where he had gone on to Trinity College from school at Winchester, when he succeeded to the dukedom in 1892.

The following year the new Duke's coming of age was celebrated. "Many years have elapsed since so large a house party had been entertained at Blenheim," gushed *The Gentlewoman*, "and it was fully in accordance with the fitness of things that Lady Blandford [the Duke's mother] should be occupying the position of hostess." The county ball was the crowning point of the festivities, and proved, as it was intended it should, fully in accordance with the traditions of hospitality at Blenheim . . . The long suite of rooms, lit by electricity and beautifully decorated with flowers, never showed to greater advantage, whilst the Long Library, which

Opposite: "Sunny aged 3 or 4"; the caption is written by his second wife, Gladys Deacon. The future 9th Duke is wearing the model uniform of the Oxfordshire Hussars, with whom he was to serve for many years.

The celebrations for the 9th Duke of Marlborough's sixtieth (or as it was belatedly ascertained, fifty-ninth) birthday at Blenheim.
Left: Estate workers pile up the bonfire with the aid of a ladder.
Below: Oxford undergraduates toast the Duke's health.

did duty as a ballroom, was the finest sight of all.

The gardens glittered with fairy lanterns and were illuminated by fireworks. Christ Church undergraduates, banned from attending the fiesta by a tiresome Dean, painted "the House" (the college, not the palace) red in protest, with the legend "Damn the Dean". F. E. Smith, then an undergraduate at Wadham and a lifelong friend of Sunny's, greatly enjoyed himself. He claimed to have kidnapped one of the Duke's valuable grey blood horses to pull him back to Oxford in a hansom cab that had lost its own steed to another undergraduate and its driver to drink. "Next morning," said F.E., "the horse was sent surreptitiously back to Blenheim – accompanied by the strongest injunctions of silence, and tips for which I had considerable difficulty in borrowing the money."

Whatever the truth of this unlikely tale, the occasion seemed to augur a new golden age at Blenheim. The new Duke, a gifted, scholarly young man of taste and artistic imagination cared passionately for the palace and understood its point. "Blenheim," he was to write in 1914, "is the most splendid relic of the age of Anne, and there is no building in Europe except Versailles, which so perfectly preserves its original atmosphere." From the start he longed to make good the depredations Blenheim had suffered but where was the cash going to come from?

The answer, of course, was America. Like his father before him, he needed an heiress with "plenty of tin". The ambitious Mrs Vanderbilt, wife of the multi-millionaire railroad tycoon, "W.K.", was all too ready to push her daughter Consuelo (presciently named after an earlier dollar duchess, Her Grace of Manchester) in Sunny's direction – and to make sure she stayed pushed. This was to be one of the last examples of a blatantly "arranged" marriage. Alva Vanderbilt wanted a Duke for her daughter; Sunny Marlborough wanted the money for his palace.

"He had a small aristocratic face with a large nose and rather prominent blue eyes," was Consuelo's impression of Sunny when they met for the first time during the London season of 1893. "His hands, which he used in a fastidious manner, were well shaped and he seemed inordinately proud of them." That autumn, back in America, Consuelo fell in love with Winthrop Rutherfurd, a perfectly respectable catch to anyone but the awful Alva whose heartless behaviour in blocking the romance recalls a melodramatic novelette. On a later visit to Blenheim Sunny showed Consuelo round the estate, as she recalled in her marvellous memoirs, *The Glitter and the Gold*:

> It was that afternoon that he must have made up his mind to marry me and to give up the girl he loved, as he told me so tragically soon after our marriage. For to live at Blenheim in the pomp and circumstance he considered essential needed money, and a sense of duty to his family and to his tradition

indicated the sacrifice of personal desires.

When I left Blenheim after that week-end I firmly decided that I would not marry Marlborough.

But the die was cast and eventually in November 1896 Consuelo, her eyes swollen with the tears she had wept alone that morning, was virtually frog-marched through the motions of becoming the Duchess of Marlborough. Sunny collected $2.5 million in 50,000 shares of capital stock of the Beech Creek Railway Company, on which an annual payment – for life – of 4 per cent was guaranteed by Vanderbilt's New York Central Railway Company.

The saltier side of the American press enjoyed themselves: "Miss Consuelo Vanderbilt and the Duke of Marlborough will be married before the end of the year," announced the *Toledo Blade*, "the date of the divorce is yet uncertain." The *Washington Post* observed that "The roof of the Marlborough Castle will now receive some much needed repairs and the family will be able to go back to three meals a day."

Arriving in London after an extended wedding tour while Blenheim was renovated in readiness for the new Duchess, Consuelo was taken along to Grosvenor Square to be inspected by Sunny's formidable grandmother, Dowager Duchess Fanny. The old crone expressed the hope that she would see Blenheim restored to its former glories (which, incidentally, her husband had done so much to diminish) and the prestige of the family upheld. Then fixing her cold grey eyes on Consuelo, the Dowager said: "Your first duty is to have a child and it must be a son, because it would be intolerable to have that little upstart Winston become Duke. Are you in the family way?"

Consuelo was indeed and did her duty as a Duchess by producing not just one heir but two: John Albert Edward William ("Bert"), Marquess of Blandford (modelled in bronze as a baby by Fuchs, a faintly embarrassing work now displayed in the Second State Room) and his younger brother, Lord Ivor Spencer-Churchill. The family were painted by her great compatriot John Singer Sargent in 1905; the immensely stylish group is by no means overshadowed by the Reynolds of the 4th Duke and his brood that hangs opposite it in the Red Drawing-Room. Like his ancestor, the 9th Duke is attired in Garter robes (he was knighted in the Order in 1900), while Consuelo, at Sargent's suggestion, wore "a black dress whose wide sleeves were lined with deep rose satin"; it was modelled on the dress Mrs Killigrew is wearing in the painting by Van Dyck which hangs in the same room. Among the other likenesses of the beautiful, sad, swan-necked Consuelo at Blenheim are a white marble bust by the American sculptor Waldo Story in the corridor leading from the Great Hall to the Long Library) and Carolus Duran's wistful portrait in the First State Room. "My mother," recalled Consuelo, "wished my portrait to bear comparison with those of preceding Duchesses

Sunny shortly before he succeeded to the dukedom of Marlborough in 1892.

Right: An American cartoonist's view of the Marlboroughs' penchant for dollar duchesses.

Following their wedding tour, Sunny and Consuelo arrive at Blenheim, 31 March 1896. The horses were later unhitched from the carriage and, as Consuelo recalled, "our employees proceeded to drag us up to the house". The new American Duchess's "democratic principles rebelled" at this means of progress.

who had been painted by Gainsborough, Reynolds, Romney and Lawrence. In that proud and lovely line I still stand over the mantelpiece . . . with a slightly disdainful and remote look as if very far away in thought."

The nightly ritual of dining alone with Sunny proved particularly trying for Consuelo:

How I learned to dread and hate these dinners, how ominous and wearisome they loomed at the end of a long day. They were served with all the accustomed ceremony, but once a course had been passed the servants retired to the hall; the door was closed and only a ring of the bell placed before Marlborough summoned them. He had a way of piling food on his plate; the next move was to push the plate away, together with knives, forks, spoons and glasses – all this in considered gestures which took a long time; then he backed his chair away from the table, crossed one leg over the other and endlessly twirled the ring on his little finger. While accomplishing these

gestures he was absorbed in thought and quite oblivious of any reactions I might have . . . As a rule neither of us spoke a word. I took to knitting in desperation and the butler read detective stories in the hall.

In the hierarchy of indoor servants, it was the butler who headed the list of precedence. Next came the groom of the chambers; the Duke's valet; the under-butler, three or four footmen (all at least six foot tall with powdered hair, maroon plush breeches, maroon coats, waistcoats with silver braid, flesh-coloured silk stockings and silver-buckled shoes); and some "odd" men whose duties included washing all the windows once a year. On the distaff side, there was the housekeeper; the Duchess's maid; a noticeably inadequate contingent of half-a-dozen housemaids who lived in the "Heights"; five laundresses and a still-room maid. In the kitchen a French chef presided over a staff of four and then there was the nursery where Nanny Marlborough held sway.

In The Glitter and the Gold, *Consuelo said of her homecoming: "The whole countryside had turned out to greet us . . . Tenant farmers, employees and household servants were ranged in groups, and each had prepared a welcoming speech and a bouquet . . ." Note the American flag, the guard of honour from the Oxfordshire Hussars and the servants watching from the roof of the colonnade.*

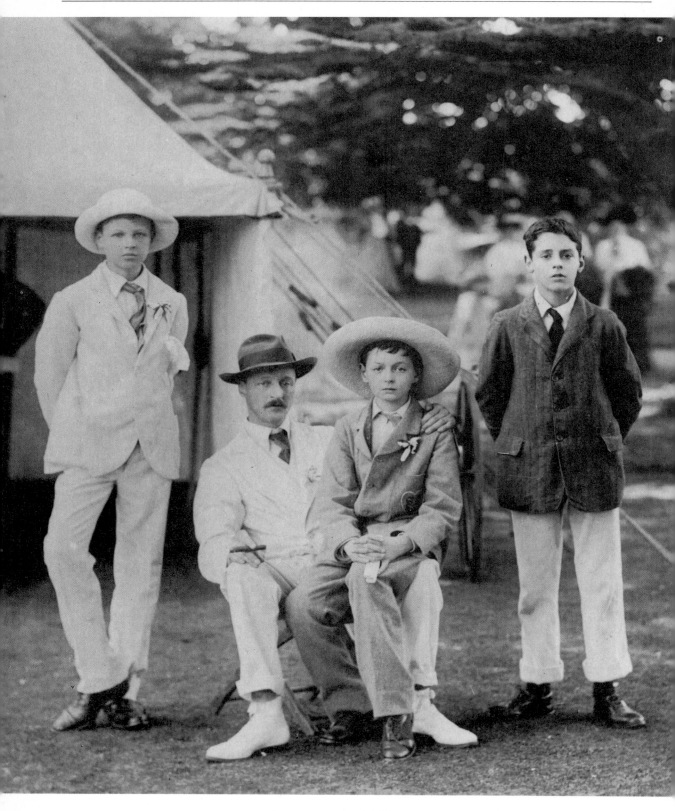

Sunny, seated, with his younger son, Lord Ivor Spencer-Churchill on his knee and his elder son, Lord Blandford ("Bert") on his right.

The inside staff at Blenheim amounted to about forty in these opulent days before the First World War. For a time a black Egyptian page was added to the strength, much to Consuelo's discomfort as he tended to follow her about:

> In his Oriental costume and turban he looked picturesque, but he was a perpetual cause of irritation, for his garbled messages in broken English caused endless misunderstandings. When he threatened an old lady who sold toys in the village, brandishing a knife and shouting that he would kill her if she did not reimburse him for the objects he had broken and wished to return, I was glad of an excuse to send him back to his native land.

During house parties, the numbers of servants greatly increased, the men visitors bringing grooms and valets, and the ladies their maids, and often a special footman to clean their boots and shoes.

Outside, the staff numbered forty to fifty. Sunny maintained a hunting department at Bladon with a staff of a dozen; the equine complement was twenty grey hunters and twenty bay carriage horses. The chief electrician had four men under him and there were carpenters, decorators (literally flower-arrangers), a dairy-man and a dairymaid, a night-watchman and a police dog (an Airedale in those days), lodge keepers (dressed in black coats with silver buttons, buff breeches and gaiters, a cockaded top hat, and carrying a long staff . . .), and a cricket professional to coach the Duke and his family. The score of gamekeepers were attired in green velvet coats with brass buttons, and black billy-cock hats.

The first big shooting party Sunny and Consuelo gave at Blenheim was for the Prince and Princess of Wales in 1896. Arthur Balfour, the politician, gave a sardonic guest's eye view to his friend and fellow-member of that high-minded group known as the "Souls", Lady Elcho:

> There is here a big party in a big house in a big park beside a big lake. To begin with (as our Toast lists have it) "the Prince of Wales and the rest of the Royal family . . ." Or if not quite that at least a quorum, namely himself, his wife, two daughters and a son-in-law. There are two sets of George Curzons, the Londonderrys, Grenfells, Gosfords, H. Chaplin, etc., etc. We came down by special train – rather cross most of us – were received with illuminations, guards of honour, cheering and other follies, went through agonies about our luggage, but finally settled down placidly enough.
>
> Today the men shot and the women dawdled. As I detest both occupations equally I stayed in my room till one o' clock and then went exploring on my bike, joining everybody at luncheon. Then, after the inevitable photograph, I again be-took myself to my faithful machine . . . You perceive the duties of society are weighing lightly upon me.

BLENHEIM REVISITED

The shooting party outside High Lodge during the visit of the Prince and Princess of Wales in 1896. Back row (left to right): the Earl of Gosford, Lady Emily Kingscote, Sidney Greville, George Curzon, General Ellis, the Countess of Gosford, Arthur Balfour, Mrs Willy Grenfell, Sir Samuel Scott, the Marquess of Londonderry, Lady Helen Stewart, Lady Lilian Spencer-Churchill, Willy Grenfell, Prince Charles of Denmark and Viscount Curzon. Middle row: the Earl of Chesterfield, Lady Randolph Churchill, the Duchess of Marlborough (Consuelo), the Princess of Wales, Harry Chaplin, the Prince of Wales, Mrs George Curzon, the Marchioness of Londonderry, Princess Victoria and Princess Charles of Denmark. Front row: Lady Sophie Scott, the Duke of Marlborough (Sunny) and Viscountess Curzon.

The "inevitable photograph", a classic of its kind and much reproduced, was taken outside High Lodge where lunch was served. The Princess (later Queen Alexandra) made her hostess laugh by her description of how she had to use a ladder in order to get into Consuelo's bed – the Marlboroughs' private apartments on the ground floor of the east wing were vacated for royal visitors – and how she kept falling over the white bear-skins that were strewn on the floor.

Gerald Horne, a hall boy at the time of the royal visit, recalled the view from the balcony of the Great Hall where the assembled house party of thirty-six were dining at one long table:

I went up and looked down and there it all was, all gleaming with wealth. I think the first thing that struck me was the flashing headgear of the ladies. The Blue Hungarian [the band which regularly came down from London to Blenheim] was playing and there was the Prince himself looking really royal and magnificent in military uniform. The table was laid of course with the silver-gilt service . . . the royal footmen waiting side by side with our own.

For the luncheon given to the Kaiser in the summer of 1899 the Saloon was used. Afterwards the German Emperor, whose

"undistinguished appearance" in mufti surprised Consuelo, regaled the company with a lecture on the military achievements of the 1st Duke of Marlborough and Prince Eugène of Savoy as they toured the State Rooms. In the Library Wilhelm clapped heartily after the organist, Mr Perkins from Birmingham, had played the Kaiser's own composition *San an Aegir* and other German pieces, and later issued an invitation to him to give a royal command performance in Berlin. Organ recitals were a popular feature at Blenheim house parties; the Prince of Wales particularly enjoyed the strains of Wagner booming out down the long room.

The Boer War, which marked an ominous beginning to the twentieth century, found Sunny in South Africa serving with the Oxfordshire Hussars in the field and on the staff (one of several Dukes in the entourage of Field-Marshal Lord Roberts, to whom he became Assistant Military Secretary), despite the fact that he had recently joined Lord Salisbury's last government as Paymaster-General. A staunch Imperialist and supporter of market preference for Empire products (such as cotton), he went on to become Under-Secretary of State for the Colonies under Joseph Chamberlain in his friend Arthur Balfour's administration. His finest hour was when he made a speech in the House of

The Druids' gathering at Blenheim, 1908. Surrounded by bearded ancients, stands the bow-tied figure of Winston Churchill. In the centre foreground, Sunny appears to be sitting on his straw hat.

Lords defending the government's policy of permitting Chinese labour in the Rand Mines.

Like many politicians, the Duke was not so keen on meeting the people he pontificated about in the flesh. We are given a vignette of Sunny in the memoirs of the Benedictine abbot, Sir David Hunter-Blair, who brought a party of Oxford undergraduates when the palace was open to the public. In the Saloon

the big glass doors suddenly opened, and the little Duke in khaki (he was encamped with his Yeomanry in the park) rushed in, and seeing the mob of tourists, rushed out again with a loud and forcible expletive. We all stared at this unexpected apparition, but the butler who was escorting us (looking like a duke himself) merely announced, with no sign of emotion, "His Grace, the Duke of Marlborough"!

Sunny relished the Yeomanry camps, particularly in the company of his ebullient cousin Winston Churchill and the laconic F.E. Smith. "They behaved like Regency rakes," recalled F.E.'s widow. The soldiering was not exactly arduous (F.E. would send his men up a tree in the park to see what was going on, and fall asleep underneath it) and in the evenings there would be parties in the palace – with a sort of Ruritanian full-dress uniform (including the Churchillian maroon breeches) being worn – or cosily masculine card parties in each other's tents.

"What shall we play for, F.E.?" asked Sunny one night.

"Your bloody palace if you like," replied Smith.

Despite their political differences – Sunny being a staunch Tory, Winston then a radical Liberal – the friendship of the cousins survived and Winston was a regular guest at Blenheim. He was not, however, as sometimes stated, among the guns that bagged the world record number of rabbits in a day (6,943). The three cronies, Sunny, Winston and F.E., were together at Blenheim in the summer of 1908 when, at Winston's instigation, Clementine Hozier came to stay. As her daughter and biographer, Mary Soames, relates

Before retiring to bed on the Monday evening Winston made an assignation with Clementine to walk in the rose garden the following morning after breakfast. Appearing punctually at breakfast was never at any time in his life one of Winston's more pronounced qualities; even on this day of days he was late!

Clementine came downstairs with characteristic punctuality, and was much discomfited by Winston's non-appearance. While she was eating breakfast, she seriously turned over in her mind the possibility of returning then and there to London. The Duke observed that Clementine was much put out, and took charge of the situation. He despatched a sharp, cousinly note upstairs to Winston and, deploying his utmost charm, suggested to Clementine that he should take her for a drive in his buggy. He whirled her round the estate for about half an hour, and upon their return there was the dilatory Winston anxiously scanning the horizon.

The carefully planned betrothal came about finally in the late afternoon, in the Temple of Diana, where the couple had taken refuge from a downpour. A plaque now commemorates that "In this temple Winston S. Churchill proposed to Clementine Hozier 11th August 1908." The building was restored in 1975 ("European Architectural Heritage year") by the present Duke of Marlborough and opened by Baroness Spencer-Churchill, as Clemmie became. "There was a bench there then," she recalled, "and as I sat there with Winston I watched a beetle slowly moving across the floor. 'If that beetle reaches that crack,' I said to myself, 'and Winston hasn't proposed, then he isn't going to.' But he did propose!'"

"At Blenheim," said Sir Winston, "I took two very important decisions: to be born and to marry; I am happily content with the decisions I took on both those occasions." He and Clemmie spent the first days of their honeymoon here and continued to be frequent visitors to the palace until an unfortunate incident in 1913 in the Green Drawing-Room, where the family sometimes lunched. Clemmie, staying without Winston, was handed a telegram from Lloyd George which she promptly proceeded to answer at one of the writing tables in the room. Sunny, disgruntled by the Welsh wizard's recent proposals for Land Reform, snapped: "Please, Clemmie, would you mind not writing to that horrible little man on Blenheim writing-paper." Whereupon the fiercely loyal political wife returned immediately to London and a temporary coolness ensued between Clemmie and Sunny.

Sunny's own treatment of women was certainly not his strongest suit. He emerges as a deeply unsympathetic character from both Consuelo's *The Glitter and The Gold* and Hugo Vickers's remarkable biography of his second wife, *Gladys, Duchess of Marlborough*. Sunny and Consuelo decided to go their separate ways in 1906, the Duchess establishing herself at Sunderland House in Mayfair. According to Lord Hugh Cecil, Sunny took the view "that his wife is unfit to live with him because she went wrong before he did and because the standard of women in these things is higher than for men." Even if Consuelo was unfaithful (and one can hardly blame her), such an attitude earned Sunny scant respect. Just as in the previous generation, the Marlboroughs were effectively banished from court circles (Edward VII and Queen Alexandra making it clear that they would take a very dim view of divorce); while in America the President, Teddy Roosevelt, spoke for many in a letter to Whitelaw Reid:

I thoroly dislike . . . these international marriages . . . But the lowest note of infamy is reached by such a creature as this Marlborough, who proposing to divorce the woman when *he* at least cannot afford to throw any stone at her, nevertheless proposes to keep and live on the money she brought him, come my dear Sir . . . surely you don't object to my considering the Duke of Marlborough a cad!

In the end Sunny and Consuelo were not divorced until 1921, both remarrying within a few weeks of the decree absolute. Consuelo married a French aviator, Lieutenant-Colonel Jacques Balsan and settled in France, while her old friend and compatriot, Gladys Deacon (described by Consuelo as "a beautiful girl endowed with a brilliant intellect") became the new Duchess of Marlborough and *châtelaine* of Blenheim.

Sunny had first met Gladys (pronounced "Glaydus", incidentally) in London back in 1897 when she was only sixteen. Of Bostonian background and cosmopolitan childhood, Gladys seems to have stepped out of the pages of a Henry James novel. The diarist Chips Channon described her as "the toast of Paris . . . the *belle amie* of Anatole France"; Robert de Montesquiou as "the marvel" and Marcel Proust "never saw a girl with such beauty, such magnificent intelligence, such goodness and charm". She was an intimate at I Tatti (its owner, the art historian Bernard Berenson being one of the many who sought her hand), a close friend of Rodin and Degas. At the age of twenty-two, Gladys, in search of the perfect Grecian profile, had paraffin wax injected into the bridge of her nose. Unfortunately the wax later slipped down inside her face to her chin, giving her an unsightly pouch under her jaw. Despite this blow to her beauty, she was to enchant an astonishing list of suitors ranging from the Dukes of Norfolk and Camastra to the philosopher Keyserling; Gladys's other close friends included Jacob Epstein (who was to sculpt both her and Sunny) and Queen Victoria's last surviving son, the Duke of Connaught.

Like Sunny, Gladys had experienced a traumatic childhood. At the age of eleven her father shot her mother's lover in an hotel room at Cannes. Curiously enough, three years later, the adolescent Miss Deacon was regretting she had been too young to catch Sunny, whose first American bride was a neighbour of Gladys's family in the fashionable resort of Newport, Rhode Island. As things turned out she had to endure a long wait.

Gladys Deacon stayed regularly at Blenheim in Consuelo's time and in 1901 her dalliance with the German Crown Prince during his visit to the palace (following in the footsteps of his father, the Kaiser) caused an international sensation. According to *Le Matin*, love burgeoned between Gladys and the Crown Prince (known as "Little Willy" and described by Consuelo as having a silly, degenerate expression) as the sun set on a perfect summer evening and a game of tennis drew to its close. Little Willy, a susceptible youth, impulsively pledged his love with the ring his mother had given him for his first communion, while Gladys handed over her bracelet. When the Kaiser learnt of the ring's absence he sent a furious message through his chamberlain to Consuelo, demanding its immediate return. Gladys surrendered it, somewhat reluctantly, and duly received back her bracelet. Towards the end of his life Little Willy wistfully recollected that there had once been a charming American whom he would have much liked to marry but the Kaiser had forbidden the match.

A mutually attractive third party often helps to sustain a marriage and the Marlboroughs fawned on Gladys. On one day in 1904 both wrote to her in glowing terms after she had been ill. Sunny spoke of the "deepest and finest devotion" he felt for Gladys "for kindness which I believe few men have received at a woman's hands . . . a heart kinder and more sensitive than any I have known"; while Consuelo (or "Coon") drooled: "women can give to each other what no man gives us . . . I have never cared for any other woman like you." There was emphatically no question of Gladys playing any part in the break-up of the Duke of Marlborough's first marriage. Indeed their relationship did not apparently develop into full-blown intimacy until some five years after Sunny's separation from Consuelo. Sunny's principal concern during this period was the resurgence of Blenheim upon which he set his heart.

In the years between succeeding to the dukedom in 1892 and the First World War – in effect, *la belle époque* – the 9th Duke of Marlborough carried out his first set of labours at Blenheim. These included the restoration of the original formality to the Great Court (French granite-setts replacing the grass that had come to make the front of the palace look more like a hayfield than a *cour d'honneur*); the dredging of the lake; the replanting of the Grand Avenue in the park beyond the Column of Victory; and the creation of a new formal garden on the original site of Duchess Sarah's ill-fated flower garden by the east wing of the palace. Inside, Sunny's new broom swept away some of the Victorian gloom; the remaining treasures were sympathetically rearranged and added to; the Library fitted up once more with bookcases and some books to go on them. After the First World War was to come the creation of the majestic Water Terraces on the west front. North, east and west, then, were all superbly improved by Sunny; the hoped-for restoration of the Great Parterre to the south, alas, proved beyond his scope and resources. Caddish he may have been to continue to accept Consuelo's cash, but without it Blenheim could have been ruined.

The perfectionist Sunny came to regret his early redecoration of the three State Rooms to the west of the Saloon – that is to say

In the 1920s Duchess Gladys, Sunny's second wife, recorded the creation of the water terraces to the west of the palace with her camera.
Left: Instant trees. The gardeners prepare to install another full-grown tree with the aid of ''Barrow's Transplanting Machine''.

Sunny's French architect and landscape designer, Achille Duchêne (in Homburg hat and velvet-collared overcoat) supervises the digging of the first water terrace.

Above: Sunny and his head gardener review progress up on the first terrace, while, underneath them, the men excavate the second terrace, piling the earth into wagons on a custom-built railway.

Right: Venus is trussed up for hoisting into position on the first terrace.

Above: One of Blenheim's great masterpieces,
Raphael's Madonna degli Ansidei, *sold by the*
8th Duke of Marlborough.

Right: Consuelo dominates a corridor in the
private apartments of the palace.

the First, Second and Third State Rooms – with their Versailles-inspired *boiseries* (gilded woodwork). "When I was young and uninformed," he said, "I put French decoration into the three state rooms here. The rooms have English proportions . . . and the result is that the French decoration is quite out of scale . . . and leaves a very unpleasant impression on those who possess trained eyes." While conceding it may be sad that such famous rooms were altered, the distinguished art historians Robin Fedden and John Kenworthy-Browne comment in *The Country House Guide* that "the pastiche is accomplished and the craftsmanship meticulous."

Sunny's somewhat hypercritical reflections on his early handiwork were addressed to his major collaborator in the resurgence of Blenheim, the French architect and landscape designer Achille Duchêne. "You will remember," the Duke wrote to Duchêne some years later, "how we noticed that Monsieur Brown, being pleased with having made a Lake, raised the soil over the old Court Yard, thinking thereby to show off his Lake better. You rebuilt that Court Yard and so well did you do it that no one has ever suspected that it did not form part of the original building." This was certainly a richly-deserved compliment from a man not always ready with an encouraging word. Between 1900 and 1910 the three-acre forecourt was entirely repaired according to Vanbrugh's original plan. Sunny even thought of taking the opportunity to erect Vanbrugh's proposed Great Gate and colonnades which would have enclosed the forecourt but this was, perhaps wisely, considered over-ambitious. The present parapet, sunk wall and iron gates were put up instead.

On the east front Sunny had the Victorian shrubbery torn up and commissioned Duchêne, a disciple of Louis XIV's great landscapist, Le Nôtre, to create a formal garden bordered on two sides by the Orangery and the private apartments. Although known as the Italian Garden, the result, with its exquisitely fashioned evergreen topiary and luscious little orange trees, resembles more of a French *jardin d'honneur*. The centrepiece of the garden, the gilded Mermaid fountain, is a work of remarkable panache by the Anglophile American Waldo Story, the sculptor who was also responsible for the marble busts of Sunny and Consuelo in the north-west corridor of the palace.

Capability Brown is sometimes blamed for destroying all formality in the grounds of Blenheim in favour of "naturalism" but, to be fair to him, he did, for the sake of contrast, retain some formal landscape features in the park, such as the Grand Avenue and the radiating avenues south-east of the palace. Sadly, in the course of the nineteenth century these features were removed as Brown's designs matured. Between 1902 and 1905 Sunny replanted the two-mile-long Grand Avenue from the Column of Victory to the Ditchley Gate with various species of elm, placing a square plinth in the middle. The plinth has now gone and so

too, alas, have the elms – infected by the terrible Dutch Elm disease in the mid-1970s that turned so many noble parks into versions of the lost world.

The Blenheim Fire Brigade on parade in front of the Chapel colonnade, before the First World War.

The 9th Duke, whose grandson has replaced the dead elms along the Grand Avenue with lime trees, could not have foreseen such a disaster and happily in other respects his schemes for the park have ensured that its structure can survive the ravages of disease and senility. The massive replanting undertaken in the 9th Duke's time was boldly conceived. Sunny introduced a system of new circular clumps, interspersed behind plantations, which are now coming to maturity as Capability's are collapsing from old age. A noted feature of the replantings was Sunny's insistence on more ornamental colours for the park; "the two colours, the copper and the grey, ought to be the most effective and picturesque", he observed about Bladon Piece in 1896.

Dressed in breeches and his favourite green coat, lined with rabbit fur, Sunny liked to spend the day riding or walking around the estate. It was his kingdom and he enjoyed the power of a Renaissance prince. When F.E. Smith pointed out that he had a feudal mind, Sunny did not demur. "I must be faithful to my name," he replied.

Left: John Singer Sargent's immensely stylish group of the 9th Duke of Marlborough and his family, which hangs in the Red Drawing-Room. Sunny wears his Garter robes. Bert (the future 10th Duke) stands in front of Consuelo; his younger brother, Ivor, to their mother's right.

Above: The Italian cradle, presented by Mrs W. K. Vanderbilt, in which Consuelo rocked her two sons. It now stands in the First State Room, west of the Saloon, in front of the tapestry depicting the 1st Duke of Marlborough's advance on the Schellenberg fortress.

Blenheim was – and indeed to a significant extent still is – a world apart. It had its own electricity plant, waterworks and even a fire brigade drawn from estate workers. On one occasion the men were called out in the middle of a game of cricket on the south lawn. Fire thus stopped play but within an hour the flames had been extinguished and the game could resume. Sid Jakeman has a report docket of the Blenheim Fire Brigade which categorizes penalties for such peccadilloes as "Belt or tunic improperly fastened" or "Touching the work after its completion before receiving permission". The 1906 docket, listing a dozen men under the command of H. Scroggs and including Sid's redoubtable father Tom Jakeman, records that 2,300 feet of canvas hose was used for the fire at Mr Parker's farm at Long Hanborough:

> Called by telephone from Coombe Mill at 7.15 pm. Proceeded at once with Steam Fire Engine. Arrived at 7.45. Found 2 Straw Ricks were alight in the centre of Rick Yard. Surrounded by 6 other Ricks and Farm Buildings. Found supply of water from Pond about ½ mile away . . . Confined Fire to Straw Ricks. Left all Perfectly Safe at 1.30. Arrived home at 2 o'clock.

The date was 5 November.

Every Friday morning at ten o'clock the Duke would hold what he called a council meeting in the farms office for his numerous farm baliffs. The Duke demanded progress reports from each in turn about his cattle, sheep, pigs and poultry; if the replies were not satisfactory, as one of his agents recalled, "a storm arose at once". The meetings would often go on well into the afternoon. The question of a hot luncheon becoming cold was never allowed to interrupt the proceedings but then, of course, the Duke's own food in the palace was almost invariably cold anyway – having to travel about 100 yards from kitchen stove to dining-room table.

In agricultural matters Sunny was not at all old-fashioned, carrying out what *The Times* described as "many experiments of great value to the working farmer". In 1913 he put a thousand acres of the park under the plough. He wanted to demonstrate, as he said, that "with wheat at the price of 4s. a bushel, or 32s. a quarter, it would pay the community to put back under the plough the land which was turned into rather poor pasture during the time of the depression." The experiment proved a success in that the land yielded a better return from wheat than from pasturage.

During the First World War Sunny intensified his agricultural activities, substituting sheep for mowers in the palace gardens and growing cabbages in the flower-beds. "The national food problem may not have been greatly lessened by these practices," wrote *The Times*, "but it was a patriotic gesture." He also placed 500 head of cattle at the disposal of Lord Rhondda, the Food Controller, to relieve the shortage of meat.

In the early part of the war Sunny rejoined the colours, serving as a Lieutenant-Colonel on the General Staff and in the last year of hostilities he returned once more to government office as Joint Parliamentary Secretary to the Board of Agriculture. This job came to a somewhat awkward conclusion when, in his private capacity as owner of Blenheim, he failed to see eye to eye with the Board's local officials who were sent to tell him what to do with his own land. In 1915 he had become Lord-Lieutenant of Oxfordshire. The appointment, as the representative of the King (now George V) in the county, meant a lot to Sunny as a mark of renewed favour with what would now be called "the Establishment". "I really believe this is the first letter I have written to you since you became Lord-Lieutenant," purred Sir Herbert Warren, the legendarily snobbish President of Magdalen. "Perhaps it is not inappropriate that I should now, if it is not too late, tell you how much pleased I was about that, for it was an additional touch that these distinguished guests [some French professors Warren was trying to impress] should be entertained, not only by the Duke of Marlborough, but by the Lord-Lieutenant of Oxfordshire."

Sunny had had to fight hard to secure the Lieutenancy against some spiteful intrigue by Consuelo, who pushed forward the claims of the Marquess of Lansdowne to the Liberal Prime Minster, Mr Asquith (regarded as an old sot by Sunny). After Sunny had told "Little L" where he could get off (perhaps employing the expletive that so diverted Abbot Hunter-Blair and his flock), Winston, F.E. and their gang of bruisers helped to win the day for the Duke.

F.E. continued to tease his melancholy, highly-strung old friend. "Do you know," the Duke once complained to another peer, "that he ridiculed my insisting on my guests wearing white ties at Blenheim, and also complained that my habit of signing myself 'Marlborough' even to my dearest friends, who in conversation would call me 'Sunny', displayed a pompous mind? I am afraid that poor F.E. does not understand that people in certain positions have to maintain a certain dignity."

Sometimes, though, Sunny saw the joke. When he told F.E. that the biggest bore in London was coming to stay in order to render useful advice on the subject of reinforced concrete, the ebullient jurist offered to produce a bigger bore within a radius of ten miles from Blenheim, and to back him in a contest F.E.

dug out a crony from his Oxfordshire Yeomanry days whose subject was fox-hunting in all its aspects, and he was confident enough to wager £10 on him against the cement expert. F.E. told his nominee that his opponent's main interest was fox-hunting – "It is his passion" – and he told the other competitor that the Oxfordshire Yeoman was keenly interested in problems of reinforced concrete.

Opposite: Bert, the future 10th Duke, as a baby, sculpted by Emil Fuchs. The bronze is on display in the Second State Room, which is adorned with the Bouchain Tapestry of Marlborough breeching the "ne-plus-ultra" lines.

Above: The perfect Grecian features of Sunny's second wife, Gladys, on the face of one of the Blenheim sphinxes. Both sphinxes, a pair, were executed in lead by W. Ward Willis, completed in 1930 and placed opposite each other on the water terraces.

Left: Portrait of Gladys Deacon by Paul Helleu, 1901. The artist described her as "the adorable creature".

The inscription on the gate reads:

UNDER THE AUSPICES OF A MUNIFICENT SOVEREIGN THIS HOUSE WAS BUILT FOR JOHN DUKE OF MARLBOROUGH, AND HIS DUCHESS SARAH, BY SIR J.VANBRUGH BETWEEN THE YEARS 1705 AND 1722. AND THIS ROYAL MANOR OF WOODSTOCK, TOGETHER WITH A GRANT OF £240,000, TOWARDS THE BUILDING OF BLENHEIM WAS GIVEN BY HER MAJESTY QUEEN ANNE AND CONFIRMED BY ACT OF PARLIAMENT 13 & 4 ANNE C.4 TO THE SAID JOHN DUKE OF MARLBOROUGH AND TO ALL HIS ISSUE MALE AND FEMALE LINEALLY DESCENDING.

A gatekeeper stands sentinel outside the gates by Flagstaff Lodge (from where the Duke of Marlborough's standard flies when he is in residence). Vanbrugh's severe East Gate was cheered up by Sir William Chambers in 1773. The inscription ("Under the auspices of a munificent sovereign . . .") was added by the 9th Duke. The massive gates, by Bramah, were put on show at the Great Exhibition of 1851.

Thus briefed, they were left alone together for half an hour, and when the doors were opened the London visitor was found to be asleep – his opponent leaning eagerly forward and saying: "You think I went through the gate – I didn't: I went over the stile – and now I am going to tell you why."

The Smiths and the Winston Churchills were frequently of the party for Christmas at Blenheim. "Our pulses quickened every year as we left the torpid streets of Woodstock and passed under the first grey arch into the domain of the Duke of Marlborough," recalled Freddie Birkenhead in his life of his father. Sometimes the great lake was frozen and the woods white with winter, and on the wooded eyot in the centre of the lake the trees were powdered with rime, and skates rang on the ice. One passed through arch after arch before turning to the left and approaching the vast front of the building . . . there was in it an atmosphere and scent that none of us could forget. Inside the great hall with its painted ceiling, the housekeeper, Mrs Ryman, stood waiting, a bunch of keys at her waist, to take us to rooms with memorable names – Godolphin Rooms, Dean Jones Rooms, some with great four-poster beds and dark tapestries.

There were the pictures of horses we gazed upon with awe, dominated by two tremendous patriarchs, the Godolphin Arabian, and the Bloody-shouldered Arabian. There were the State-rooms with the tapestries of the Battle of Blenheim, the Duke on his rearing horse, the white puffs of artillery, and the serried ranks of the opposing forces.

Every aspect of this house, which occupies three acres of land, filled us with excitement and invited exploration – the great hall with its radiators on which we lay on our backs and gazed at the painted ceiling, at the royal blue sky and the gods and goddesses, the dark turreted stairs leading to unexpected places. There was the Long Library with that elusive scent, compound of heaven knows what subtle combination of ingredients, the library with its white statue of Queen Anne – and at the end the Willis organ rearing itself above the bookcases . . .

Strewn round this great room were white bearskin rugs on which we lay while Perkins, the organist from Birmingham, indifferent to the political arguments of the adults and the noises of the children, sat by the hour immersed in his own world, playing Bach fugues and improvising themes.

A house party at Blenheim photographed by Duchess Gladys, July 1923. Among the guests are, on the left, "F.E." (the Earl of Birkenhead) and Winston Churchill; and (fifth from left, middle row) Lytton Strachey. The tall moustachioed figure in the centre is Earl Fitzwilliam. Sunny stands by the pillar to the right.

Overleaf (left): Duchêne's plans for the water terraces to the west of the palace and a recent photograph. "If you study this picture and compare it with the finished work . . ." boasted Sunny, "you will realize . . . how I succeeded in destroying the French middle-class view of a formal garden." Overleaf (right): Bernini's fountain, a model of the River Gods Fountain in Rome's Piazza Navona, on the second terrace.

IF YOU STUDY THIS PICTURE AND COMPARE IT WITH THE
FINISHED WORK ON THE TERRACES, YOU WILL REALISE
THE IMMENSE INFLUENCE I HAD OVER THE ARCHITECT
IN MAKING THE EFFECT OF THE TERRACE CLASSICAL IN
APPEARANCE, AND HOW I SUCCEEDED IN DESTROYING THE
FRENCH MIDDLE CLASS VIEW OF A FORMAL GARDEN.
MARLBOROUGH

CHATEAU DE BLENHEIM

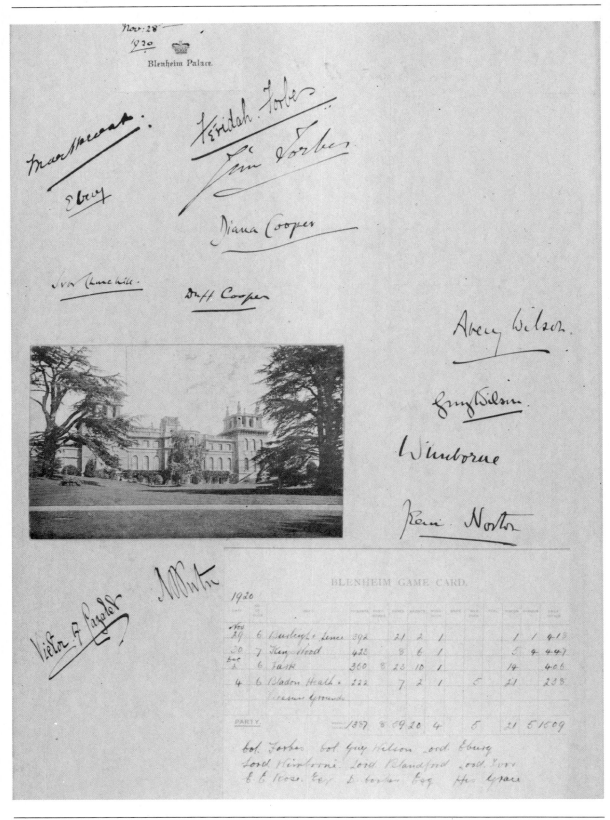

When F.E.'s family arrived at Blenheim each Christmas his entourage consisted of four hunters for F.E., two for his wife, two ponies, three grooms, two nurses, a maid and a valet. All the other guests took the same equipment, and it is worth observing that on at least one occasion a hundred people slept in the house.

Where they slept exactly was a subject best left alone. In her diary Lady Cynthia Asquith tells how Lady Diana Manners (later Cooper), that serene survivor from *la belle époque*, prepared for her début at Blenheim in 1917 at a time when she was reciving the unwelcome attentions of the Viceroy of Ireland:

> Lord Wimborne was of the party and the Duchess of Rutland, considering it a house of ill-fame, had presented Diana with a revolver and charged her to be sure and say at tea-time, in a loud voice, that her maid always slept with her! Lord Wimborne is said to have given instructions to have the locks removed from the doors!

The Duchess was proved right when the lecherous Viceroy duly effected an entry into Lady Diana's bedroom. His candle revealed a sight that gave him pause; for he was looking down the barrel of a service revolver (belonging, incidentally, to the poet Patrick Shaw-Stewart). The old lecher was then reduced to sitting at the end of Lady Diana's bed in pretence that he had just dropped in for an early-morning chat.

Randolph Churchill, Winston and Clemmie's bombastic son, was a corridor creeper of a younger generation, as his cousin Anita Leslie recalls in her memòirs *The Gilt and the Gingerbread*. She was in the bedroom of Patricia Richards, an attractive Australian girl (later the Countess of Jersey) whom Randolph had lured down to Blenheim, saying goodnight, when

> a step sounded in the corridor. Randolph had made his way from the bachelor wing. Patricia clutched me nervously. "Don't leave me," she whispered. Boldly I stepped over to the door and opened it to his knock. Randolph did not look too pleased and pulled me out into the corridor. "Look here, coz take this and go to your own room . . . " I scorned his pound note, turned back and jumped into Patricia's bed beside her. There we sat stolidly, in our nighties and dressing-gowns with cold cream on our faces and the be-ribboned slumber helmets of the day holding our short curls in place.
>
> Randolph was stymied. All he could do was ask for a corner of the eiderdown and hold forth about his future as Prime Minister. An hour passed, and then he had to go. His eyes were cold when he bade me goodnight.

Randolph himself recollected the Christmases of his youth at Blenheim as "always very splendid affairs" with "a lot of other children there; the huge park and Palace were wonderful romping grounds." Bert, who divided his time (together with

Opposite: A Blenheim shooting party, 1920. Among the guests who signed the game card were Lady Diana Cooper and her old pursuer, Lord Wimborne.

Above: The Italian Garden, on the east front of the palace (where Duchess Sarah's formal garden used to be), designed by Duchêne for the 9th Duke of Marlborough in the style of a French jardin d'honneur. *The mermaid fountain is by Waldo Story.*

Right: View of the water terraces and lake from the west front of the palace. The terraces have been compared to the Parterre d'Eau *at Versailles and constitute a remarkable twentieth-century achievement. The jets of water on the first terrace are a recent innovation of the present Duke's.*

his brother Ivor) between Blenheim and his mother's house in Mayfair, told how Winston, his brother Jack Churchill and F.E. Smith "livened things up with wild games of 'French and English' in the hall". Christmas 1918 coincided with the end of the Great War and with the delayed celebrations of Bert's coming of age. Randolph wrote in *Twenty-One Years*:

> There was a paper-chase on horse-back and a whole ox was roasted. The day concluded with a gigantic bonfire on top of which was placed an effigy of the Kaiser. I seem to remember that F.E.'s daughter, Lady Eleanor Smith, contributed a discarded pair of silk stockings. These were stuffed with straw and served as the Imperial legs.

During the war the 9th Duke of Marlborough had served not only the cause of agriculture but that of art. Under Gladys Deacon's urging he managed to prevent the sculptor Jacob Epstein from being enlisted in the army. In March 1918 he wrote to Gladys, "Well I have fixed up Epstein for you. He is to join the Canadian Forces as an artist to mould figures and make sketches in the manner he thinks best. He will therefore not get killed." Sadly, though, Sunny was unable to persuade Gladys's great friend Marcel Proust to come and stay at Blenheim, though the great novelist was touched by the Duke's suggestion that he could "stay in bed".

After the First World War, Sunny's attempt to secure his divorce from Consuelo dragged on and on until finally Jacques Balson saved the day by persuading her to marry again. In accordance with the ridiculous divorce laws of the day Sunny and Consuelo then had to go through the farce of pretending to live together once more – they managed to spend a fortnight under the same roof at her country retreat near Lingfield in Surrey. Consuelo found Crowhurst Place, an enchanting mock-Tudor manor house rebuilt on genuinely old foundations by the Edwardian architect George Crawley, a delightful contrast to Blenheim – that is when Sunny was not in temporary residence. Next, the wretched Duke was obliged to provide "grounds" by spending the requisite nocturnal hours with an unnamed woman (presumably a professional "co-respondent") at Claridges. He booked in under the alias of Spencer.

Later Consuelo had her own ordeal to face in order to obtain an annulment of the marriage by the Roman Catholic Church, without which her second marriage would not have been valid in France. It had to be proved that Consuelo had been coerced into the Marlborough marriage by her mother. This, of course, was nothing but the truth, though several Churchmen satisfied their customary craving for publicity by criticizing the annulment. "The plea of duress," sneered the American Bishop Manning, "after a quarter of a century of married life and the birth of two children would not be entertained by any civil court."

Opposite: Gladys Deacon in her wedding dress on the day she married Sunny in Paris, June 1921. The photograph is inscribed to her nanny.

À ma chère Irène
Souvenir du 25 Juin
Duchesse de ⋯

Left: A view across the Italian Garden, with its patterned beds and boxed orange trees, to the Orangery.

Above: The seldom-used grand approach to the north, or entrance, front of the palace from Vanbrugh's bridge.

Sunny and Gladys were also obstructed by the men of God in their attempts to have a religious marriage ceremony in Paris but finally the Rector of the Presbyterian Church of Scotland conducted the service on a baking summer afternoon in 1921. "We are both awfully poor," the Duke told the press when they asked about the wedding present he had given Gladys. "Oh, don't mention anything about that in the newspapers. One should not mention those things now, especially in the English press, with the miners starving. What will the miners think, reading about wedding presents, jewellery costing £50,000? It makes them dissatisfied, it creates trouble. You can say I gave the bride a motor-car as a wedding present."

And so at last Gladys Deacon became Duchess of Marlborough at the age of forty – though she knocked five years off on the marriage certificate. Her schoolgirl fantasy had come true. A cynic might say that when dreams come true they usually turn out to be nightmares.

At first, though, her honeymoon period as *châtelaine* of Blenheim was, as she later put it, "reasonably happy". The new era was marked by two formal entries in the palace Visitors' Book: "Marlborough" and "G. Marlborough". She and Sunny would sometimes ride together around the estate or go out on the lake. "The pond lilies are closed & their leaves curled at the edges", she noted after her first idyllic boat trip. "Beautiful extatic flowers! The acacias gleam all white among the green leaves." She shared a particular interest in gardens with Sunny, enthusiastically recording the changing scene with her camera.

The second stage of the 9th Duke's great labours at Blenheim began with him recalling Achille Duchêne to finish off the formal garden on the east front. Next the Frenchman produced designs for the ambitious terraces on the west front which were to be Sunny's most outstanding legacy to the palace. The scheme was for a sort of *parterre d'eau à la Versailles* to be installed in place of the shrubbery and what Gladys called the "crooked lawn" down to the lake.

"You are the Architect, I am the Duke," Sunny reminded Duchêne at one stage in their occasionally acrimonious collaboration. Ducal memoranda would sometimes be addressed in the third person:

The problem for Monsieur Duchêne is to make a liaison . . . between the façade of Vanbrugh and the water line of the lake made by Brown. To reconcile these conflicting ideas is difficult. The difficulty is not diminished when you remember that the façade of the house is limited and the line of the lake is limitless. As an example, if you turn your back to the lake and look at the façade, your parterre, basin etc. is in scale to the façade, but if you look at the same parterre from the rotunda to the lake it is out of scale with the panorama.

Duchêne was urged to put some joy and humanity into the designs. The terraces ended up as more Italian in style than French. The Duke took the credit for this, later adding a capitalized caption to Duchêne's drawing:

IF YOU STUDY THIS PICTURE AND COMPARE IT WITH THE FINISHED WORK ON THE TERRACES YOU WILL REALISE THE IMMENSE INFLUENCE I HAD OVER THE ARCHITECT IN MAKING THE EFFECT OF THE TERRACE CLASSICAL IN APPEARANCE, AND HOW I SUCCEEDED IN DESTROYING THE FRENCH MIDDLE CLASS VIEW OF A FORMAL GARDEN.

MARLBOROUGH

Well wrapped-up against the cold, Sunny inspects the somewhat less well-clad Venus, now in position on the water terraces.

The original plan of having three terraces right the way down had to be revised because of the risk of the third terrace sliding into the lake. As constructed, there are two terraces linked by a wall of caryatids and *vasques*. The Duke congratulated Duchêne on a "stroke of genius" in bringing the water line up to the first terrace which is on the same level as the Arcade Rooms underneath the Long Library. The second terrace is adorned on the one side by Bernini's fountain (a miniature version of the River Gods Fountain in the Piazza Navona in Rome), which had been given to the 1st Duke of Marlborough by the Papal Nuncio and had formerly stood down by the Grand Cascade, and on the other by an obelisk.

The marvellous result looks at its best from the Long Library where the effect of the water can be appreciated to the full. Duchêne had wanted the water to be in perpetual motion, but the Duke warned against "a vulgar display of waterworks which can be seen at any exhibition or public park". (Vulgar or not, fountains have recently been introduced in the first terrace.) The architect was, however, generously complimented by his patron. "Pray tell Monsieur Duchêne," he wrote in 1929 when the work was virtually complete, "that the ensemble of the terraces is magnificent and in my judgement far superior to the work done by Le Nôtre at Versailles. The proportion of the house, the terrace and the lake is perfect."

Sir Sacheverell Sitwell complimented Sunny on the fine effect of the terraces and urged him on to the next stage:

If a generation preceding yours plundered the house of a great number of its treasures of art, you have certainly repaired the damage in another way by completing the garden. But I am convinced that when it is finished you will feel the need of something else to do, and I am sure that the parterre . . . ought to be recreated – or at any rate laid down in some sort of patterning that would avoid all the expense of cutting and trimming incessantly . . .

It was not to be, however. From the note Sunny wrote in 1933,

Left: Archie Illingworth's photographs of Blenheim illuminated by fireworks and by floodlights.

Above: The former Head Guide recorded the scene when the queues of visitors stretched around the Great Court in the days before the flow system for visitors was perfected.

the year before his death, it is clear that he had shot his bolt with the completion of the water terraces:

> For various reasons I have not had the heart or courage to write an account of the six years of labour and study that I devoted to superintending the work on these terraces. Perhaps I will write one day. But let not the reader assume that this work was simple, that any architect could have done it. The result is the combination of brains, knowledge of technique and culture of two men working in harmony. These two men have left the park – East and West fronts of Blenheim – in perfect architectural design: a worthy frame to the Palace.

While the work had been going on Gladys spent many hours watching and photographing the progress. Her pictures show such items as ready-grown trees arriving in carts drawn by three horses, and Venuses being unceremoniously hauled down from motor-trucks to be put in place. Gladys herself is depicted on the second terrace; the faces of the two lead sphinxes, executed by H. Ward Willis and completed in 1930, show her Grecian features as they were before the ravages of the wax damaged her beauty. Her other decorative memorial at Blenheim was painted by Colin Gill on the ceiling of the great portico above the entrance to the palace. As visitors look upwards they see six ocular panels – three blue eyes, three brown. The former unmistakably belonged to Gladys, whose eyes were, in Hugo Vickers's phrase, "so blue that any description of them would be inadequate"; to help the artist with his task she climbed the scaffold to show Colin Gill a scarf of the same icy blue as her eyes. The owner of the brown eyes remains a puzzle. Sunny himself also had blue eyes and it has been said that they might be Consuelo's.

The model for the northernmost caryatid (or, strictly speaking, "canephorus") on the wall of the water terraces can be more positively, albeit prosaically, identified as Bert Timms, one of the gardeners. The story goes that Bert was walking by just as Visseau was settling down to his carving of the stone; the sculptor stopped the gardener and asked if he would pose for him. The Timms torso was obligingly revealed for posterity.

When Bert Timms caught Visseau's eye he was presumably on his way back from one of his regular stints working in tandem with Gladys on her beloved Rock Garden down by the Grand Cascade. Created by the 5th Duke as a "bold and rugged background" to his elaborate botanical schemes at the foot of the lake, the Rock Garden was comprehensively overhauled by the indomitable Duchess. Wearing a hat and gumboots, she used to spend hours toiling away, supervising the shifting of rocks, the placing of steps and the planting of saxifrages; numerous photographs in her album attest to her passion for this garden which was a mass of yellow flowers. She took a picnic lunch down there most days which she would eat at a Druid's table

*H. E. Tidmarsh's sketches of the Grand Cascade and
the Rock Garden in the Blenheim grounds.*

Bert, the 10th Duke of Marlborough and his
Duchess, Mary, in their robes for the Coronation of
George VI in 1937.
Right (above): The inscription beneath Lord
Randolph Churchill's statue in the Chapel.

Right (below): Sir Winston Churchill's coffin is
borne to Bladon churchyard, following his State
Funeral at St Paul's Cathederal, 1965.

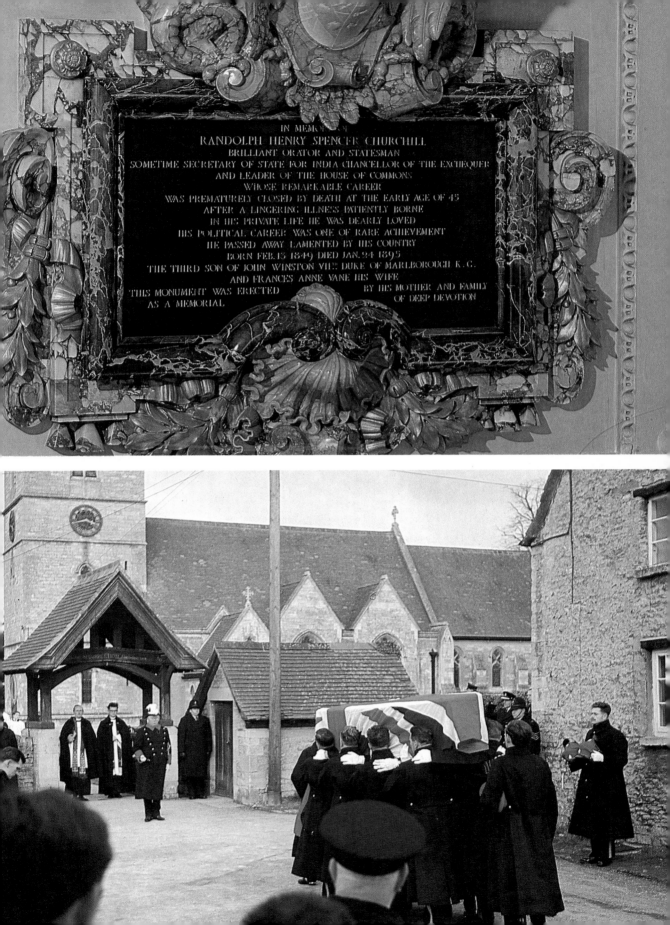

Gladys's caption to this photograph in her album reads: "Sunny's best picnic mood and expression when asked to 'look pleasant and be photographed'."

with Bert Timms or her other occasional helper, Harry Smith, a local policeman. Phon Hollis, who began work in the Blenheim gardens in the 1920s, recalls Gladys's deep voice and her habit of giving the gardeners tobacco and chocolate.

Sadly, in 1925 Gladys had to give up the industrious regime at the Rock Garden, her strength sapped by a series of miscarriages. One of them she believed to have been brought about by a squabble with Sunny in a Brighton Hotel, during which she fell against a stool. Soon after the marriage she had discovered that her dear friend of over twenty years had become a husband with an "ungovernable temper". As early as Christmas 1922 she had written

> Most interesting to me is Sunny's rudeness to me. Not very marked in public yet – but that will come. I am glad because I am sick of life here. Convention & commonplace & selfishness alone voice themselves over us. *Quelle vie!* But we will separate perhaps before long & I will then go away for good & ever.

The joy of the Rock Garden for Gladys had been its distance in terms of space and feeling from the suffocating grandeur of the palace. Gladys's friend Lily de Clermont-Tonnerre captured something of the slightly eerie, cocoon-like atmosphere when she recorded her impressions of her 1928 visit to Blenheim. The palace, she wrote was

> served by magical domestic staff, as numerous as it is invisible
> . . . I heard the fire crackling in my room without having seen it
> lighted, the curtains were drawn and breakfast was brought
> up without my being wakened, and at ten o'clock *The Times*
> was insinuated under my eyes. When I went down to the
> ground-floor, a groom of the chambers would murmur: "Her
> Grace is in the Sir Peter Lely Saloon" or in "the Long Library".
>
> By eight o'clock in the morning the lawn was rolled, the dead
> leaves removed and the flower-stands filled with fresh flowers.
>
> But this majestic silence got on my nerves, . . . those great
> mute corridors, whose never-raised voices made me homesick
> for the Latin hurly-burly . . . Blenheim Palace is protected from
> the vulgarity of democratic noises.

Gladys's old Bohemian chums hoped, in the words of the ebullient Walter Berry, to *"de-blenheimiser"*. "How can you spend *all* your days in Hyperboria?" he demanded. "What are your brain cells working on?"

Gladys's efforts to leaven the somewhat stuffy, pompous and philistine guest list did not always meet with success. The artist Jean Marchand hid in the lavatory rather than come down to dinner. When, at Gladys's suggestion, Epstein came to sculpt the Duke, the artist's casual appearance led to unfortunate misunderstandings when he was apprehended as a suspicious-looking character in the park. The sitting itself was not altogether an easy experience for either party, though the finished bust was placed in the Great Hall where it still remains. When the Duke showed the sculptor the Chapel, Epstein told his host that he could see little evidence of Christianity. The ducal response was: "The Marlboroughs are worshipped here."

The French writer André Maurois used to illustrate Anglo-Saxon attitudes by telling the story of his arrival at Blenheim. The doorkeeper referred him to a side door some distance away, but when questioned as to its exact whereabouts had to admit: "I don't know; I've never been there." Similarly, when a débutante inquired of a maid where she could find the bathroom (still notoriously in the singular) she was told "Oh miss, I wouldn't know that." In his memoirs Lord Carnarvon recalled Sunny's no-nonsense way with what the Duke uncompromisingly regarded his inferiors. During a shooting party the head game-keeper was ill and sent the Duke a message to say that he had entrusted the business of the day to his deputy. Sunny, who was incidentally a pathological hypochondriac himself, was not having any of this. "My compliments to my head keeper," he said. "Will you please inform him that the lower orders are never ill."

Aside from the expected crop of names like "Porchey"

A rare photograph of Gladys after the ravages of the wax, which she had had inserted into the bridge of her nose to give her a perfect Grecian profile.

Douglas Fairbanks, senior, the Hollywood swashbuckler of East End ancestry, hams it up with a cannon at Blenheim. His wife, Mary Pickford plays a supporting role.

Right: Jacob Epstein, the sculptor, with Sunny and the latter's head. Sir Shane Leslie thought Epstein had captured his cousin's religious spirit ("as it were a Quixote designed by Greco").

Carnarvon, the Blenheim Visitors' Book in Gladys's time reveals the occasional surprise. "They had got H.G. Wells of all people," reported Professor Lindemann after a Blenheim party in 1922, "and the Duchess made him dance, a most comic business." Lindemann himself (later Lord Cherwell), one of the Winston and F.E. set, was something of a Blenheim regular and liked to tell the story of how he had once put a Debussy roll wound the wrong way round on the pianola at the palace, persuading those listening that it was one of the French composer's less lucid pieces. (Doubtless the mention of Blenheim was "the Prof's" favourite part of the anecdote.)

Wells also turned up unannounced one weekend at Blenheim when a Greek play was being performed on the terraces. Wearying of the drama, the novelist sloped off to tea inside where Anita Leslie recalls finding him verbally jousting with Gladys.

"What I can't make out, Mr Wells, is why you are gorging in Blenheim Palace when you spend all your time decrying people who live in big houses!"

H.G. Wells, whose mother had been the housekeeper at Uppark in Sussex, beamed and stretched for another cream puff. "Well, I'll tell you. I don't mind the big houses exactly – nor people like yourself – and I never refuse a good tea . . ."

"But you haven't been invited . . ."

"No matter," continued H.G. "You interest me."

In July 1923, Lytton Strachey was among the weekend guests. He told his friend Mary Hutchinson:

Nobody was particularly interesting (except, perhaps, the Duchess) – it was the house which was entrancing, and life-enhancing. I wish it were mine. It is enormous, but one would not feel it too big. The grounds are beautiful too, and there is a bridge over a lake which positively gives one an erection. Most of the guests played tennis all day and bridge all night, so that (apart from eating and drinking) they might as well have been at Putney.

The *châtelaine* of one of Strachey's more regular haunts in that part of the world, Lady Ottoline Morrell of Garsington, found Gladys, who was never accepted by the "county", to be "the only intelligent woman in Oxfordshire".

After the abandonment of the heavy work of the Rock Garden, Gladys eventually found a new solace, like the great Duchess Sarah two centuries previously, in dogs. In 1930 Gladys revived the Blenheim spaniels, though her canine enthusiasm was not shared by Sunny. Much to his disgust, the dogs were allowed to frolic around the State Rooms; there were stories of Gladys ordering dog-flaps to be made in the doors and provoking Sunny by placing artificial dog's messes in the Long Library. By all accounts the genuine article was not in short supply either. Sunny is said to have spent hours looking for stains in the carpets

Overleaf: As they were . . . Some late-nineteenth-century interiors at Blenheim photographed by Hills & Saunders.
Left: Bedrooms (State Bed at bottom).
Right (top): Saloon, then used as a sitting-room.
Right (bottom): Red Drawing-Room, with billiard-table.

and curtains which he would then point out to bemused guests. Jack Churchill's daughter, Clarissa (who later married Anthony Eden, Earl of Avon), remembers being amazed as a child to find the Great Hall divided into coops and reeking most terribly.

In 1931 on Anita Leslie's first visit to Blenheim – the time she thwarted her cousin Randolph's nocturnal adventure – tea was held up pending the entrance of the by now increasingly eccentric hostess:

> Finally we heard, not footsteps, but the claw-clatter of many little dogs. "Watch Sunny – he hates her guts – great sport!" whispered Randolph. In came the duchess, surrounded by a moving carpet of King Charles spaniels. Gladys Marlborough was extraordinary to look at. Absolutely hideous and yet exotic, with golden hair swept back in a bun and strange blue eyes staring out of the ruin of that stretched face. She advanced in her dirty old clothes, shook hands and waved us graciously to chairs.

The warfare between Sunny and Gladys was by now out in the open. At dinner that night

> Marlborough sat looking like a rat caught in a trap, while the duchess delivered her poisoned shafts. Poor little man, I thought. He was forced to listen while his wife told us girls why we should not get married. "I didn't marry," she said, "until I'd been to bed with every prime minister in Europe – and most of the kings." The duke did not smile.

After a series of rows, at the end of that year Sunny decamped from Blenheim, leaving Gladys alone in the palace with her dogs and a reduced number of servants. The butler, under-butler, valet, chef and a kitchen-maid were whisked away by the Duke to his London house at Carlton House Terrace. Some of those who remained behind treated their mistress in a most disobliging manner, spreading rumours of her madness, drug-taking and so forth. In an atmosphere of appalling bitterness, Sunny and his agents kept up the pressure on Gladys in a campaign to make her leave. "I cannot allow my home to be used like an Hotel for ladies and gentlemen whom I may not know," telegraphed Sunny to Gladys in May 1933 after he had heard she was expecting nine guests to stay. A few weeks later Gladys decided that she had had enough, summoning a motor car and van to remove her personal things and her dogs. Before she departed, she stood on the front steps of the palace and took some photographs. Her caption to one of them reads: "Goodbye to all that!"

Sunny promptly regained possession of the palace, the squalid condition of which fuelled the legend that Gladys was "mad", and later in the summer succeeded in driving his estranged wife out of Carlton House Terrace. She was told by one of three

"Goodbye to all that!"; Gladys makes her exit from Blenheim, May 1933.

intruders, who sound like pantomime broker's men, "You have no right in this house. We are here with the Dook's orders." In her plight Gladys received a cheering note from Verena Churchill, the highly eccentric estranged wife of Sunny's cousin Victor, the 1st Viscount Churchill:

> I feel full of sympathy for you . . . I know all the ungentleman-like tricks that the family we both had the misfortune to marry into can do – the lies and spite – are you now called a lunatic as I was? – such an easy thing to say & such an unchivalrous lie to start . . . I feel so deeply for you for it is so horrible to see one's name in all the papers & unless anyone knows the ways of the Churchill family AS I DO how could anyone know the truth – I do not even have to ask about it all – for I know Churchills only fight women and children & persecute them – but never men in any position to retaliate . . . Why not leave it all & come to Paris later on – one gets so tired of all their lies and malice – But in time of course lies are shown up – It is all a question of time. "For the wheel of God grinds slowly but it grinds exceeding small" . . . I wonder if your letters are opened as mine were. If so I hope they will like this one.

Gladys faded into obscurity. During the Second World War Chips Channon encountered "an extraordinary marionette of a

Three generations at Blenheim, 1929: Sunny, the 9th Duke; Bert, the 10th Duke; and the present (11th) Duke, then aged three.

woman – or was it a man?" in a Bond Street jeweller's. As the diarist examined this "terrifying apparition" he recognized "Gladys Marlborough, once the world's most beautiful woman". Reading this passage in Chips's published diaries a quarter of a century later, Hugo Vickers became fascinated by Gladys. He discovered that the Duchess was in fact still alive, a patient in a psycho-geriatric ward. After living as a recluse in a farmhouse near Banbury for many years, she had been forcibly removed to St Andrew's Hospital, Northampton in 1962. The few who were aware of her existence had mostly long since dismissed her as a madwoman, but Vickers, who visited Gladys regularly in the last two years of her life proved otherwise in unearthing her extraordinary story.

When Gladys died in 1977 she was correctly described as the widow of the 9th Duke of Marlborough for she and Sunny, despite the ferocious cross-fire of their lawyers, had never divorced. Towards the end of his life Sunny entertained hopes of marrying for a third time but these hopes were not shared by the object of his affections, the Canadian "Bunny" Lindsay-Hogg (*née* Doble), sister-in-law of Sir Sacheverell Sitwell. Otherwise Sunny's last years were brightened by the revival of his interest in the Turf; his horse Andrea won a number of good races, and ran in the Derby.

Many valetudinarians are not only genuinely sick but also face up to real suffering with remarkable fortitude. This was the case with Sunny who died bravely of inoperable cancer of the liver (refusing morphia for as long as he remained conscious) in June 1934 aged sixty-two. The funeral was at the Jesuit church in Farm Street for, after falling out with the Church of England, Sunny had become a Roman Catholic in 1927, under the instruction of Father Martindale. At the Requiem Mass, Father Martindale spoke of Sunny's "almost disconcertingly vivid perception of the existence and primacy of the spiritual".

In the press some took a slightly less lofty view. Lord Castlerosse, the gossip columnist of the *Sunday Express*, observed that Sunny, "a pathetic figure like a lonely peacock struggling through deserted gardens", was "the last duke who firmly believed that strawberry leaves could effectively cover a multitude of sins". However, Winston Churchill, his own career in the doldrums at this stage, paid tribute to his cousin and friend in *The Times*, particularly Sunny's connoisseurship and stewardship of Blenheim:

> always there weighed upon him the size and cost of the great house which was the monument of his ancestor's victories. This he conceived to be almost his first duty in life to preserve and embellish. As the successive crashes of taxation descended upon the Old World it was only by ceaseless care and management, and also frugality, that he was able to discharge his task. He sacrificed much to this – too much; but he succeeded; and at his death Blenheim passes from his care in a finer state than ever.

After Sunny's burial in the chapel at Blenheim, Winston hailed the late Duke's elder son. *"Le duc est mort"*, he greeted the erstwhile Lord Blandford in his execrable French. *"Vive le Duc!"*

The present Duke as a boy, flanked by his sisters, Lady Sarah and Lady Caroline, both carrying Blenheim spaniels.

6. Bert

One of the more striking might-have-beens of the recent past is that if the 9th Duke of Marlborough had not had two sons, his cousin Winston Churchill would have become the 10th Duke. In these circumstances Winston would not have been Prime Minister in 1940 and modern history could well have taken a disastrously different path. After his great cousin's death in the mid-1960s, the 10th Duke wrote:

> Beyond question Blenheim made for Sir Winston the ideal background, and I don't mean only for his paintings. At times, for example when he was researching for his life of Marlborough, it must have given him inspiration; but although before I was born, he was heir to the dukedom, I doubt if he hankered much for the place itself. Much as he cared for Blenheim, it would not have appealed to him to go down in history as its owner. He had other and better ideas.

Blandford (as his first wife, Duchess Mary, always called him) was living at Lowesby Hall in Leicestershire, where he hunted regularly with the Quorn and the Cottesmore, at the time of his father's somewhat sudden and unexpected death in 1934. Shortly before his own death in 1972, the 10th Duke recalled: "I was thoroughly enjoying life when I found myself owner of Blenheim. It was rather a shock, I'll admit. I'd known it would come to me, but the suddenness was disturbing, to say the least. But one takes these things in one's stride, of course, and I soon began to take my place in local affairs." Apart from being a Deputy Lieutenant and a county councillor for Oxfordshire and High Steward of Oxford, the Duke and also the Duchess were both Justices of the Peace and served several individual terms as Mayor of Woodstock.

The Duke's sobriquet of "Bert" was a diminutive of his second Christian name "Albert". A godson of Albert Edward, Prince of Wales (later Edward VII), he had been baptized aged just under a month in October 1897 at the Chapel Royal in St James's Palace. After his parents, Sunny and Consuelo, parted when he was aged nine, he had what he described as "a somewhat divided life as a boy", spending part of his school holidays with his father at Blenheim and the rest "in the South of France, or wherever my mother happened to be staying at the time". As he was known as "The Weather Man" on account of his never-failing fascination with the vagaries of the elements (the present Duchess, a Swede,

Opposite: "Heel!" Bert and a beloved black labrador photographed by Patrick Lichfield for Life *in the 1960s.*

was touched by his insistence on telling her the temperature in Stockholm every time they met), it is appropriate that one of his early recollections of life at Blenheim revolved round the countryman's main concern. Towards the end of April 1908 he set out, complete with cricket bag, for the summer term, to go back to his private school (not called "prep schools" in those days), St Aubyn's at Rottingdean, but after a couple of miles had to turn back. "By that time the carriage was stuck in the snow," said Bert. "We measured three feet of snow at Blenheim that April."

After Eton Bert, in his own words, "graduated to the girls". As a subaltern in the Life Guards (or "Tins") and the heir to Blenheim he was obviously much in demand among the débutantes but, as he said, looking back wistfully from the 1960s, "the mothers in those days were appalling". One of them apparently locked the eligible young Marquess in a room with her daughter and asked what his inclinations were. "Of course I told her they were dishonourable," said Bert.

Like the engaging Wodehousian aristocrat he resembled in so many ways, Bert turned his attention to musical comedy actresses. Some of these thespians turned out to prefer their own sex but Bert's "particular friend" was Betty Barnes: "Oh, she was so pretty!" Bert fondly recalled, remembering the "very happy weekends with her at her cottage on Beachy Head" in between his customary mumbled refrain of "huh-huhs" and "what-whats". "When I was courting her," he said, "I used to sit in a box every night and one night my mother who disapproved, was sitting in the next box being courted by Jacques Balsan." Both Sunny and Consuelo took a dim view of their elder son's en-tanglement with Miss Barnes, especially when press posters erroneously proclaimed "MARQUESS ENGAGED TO ACTRESS". Breach of promise cases brought by chorus girls jilted by aristocratic rakes were dangerously frequent occur-rences ("Bimbo" Northampton had had to pay out as much as £50,000) and Blandford was quickly brought to heel. Sunny was inclined to ascribe these louche tastes in his son to what he regarded as the common American blood of his mother.

Like many of his generation who survived the holocaust of the "Great War" (the two Spencer-Churchill brothers both came through their active service, unlike an extraordinarily high ratio of their aristocratic friends and cousins), Bert always retained a deep sentimental attachment to the poignant popular songs of the period. One of his favourites was the recruiting ditty offering to make a man of anyone who took "the shilling". But instead of "On Sunday I go out with a soldier, on Monday I go out with a tar", Bert would sing the lewd military version beginning "On Sunday I kissed her on the ankle on Monday . . . ". He never lost his infectiously crude schoolboy sense of humour which enabled him to see a hilarious double entendre in almost everything;

often the atrocious scatological joke he was spluttering about to himself, however, would be lost to all save those with the very dirtiest minds.

Having torn himself away from the stage door, Bert married Mary Cadogan in 1920. Described by Daphne Fielding (formerly the Marchioness of Bath) as "a typical English rose even down to the thorns", Mary was very much the stuff of which Duchesses are made. A collateral descendant of Lord Cadogan, the 1st Duke of Marlborough's faithful lieutenant at Blenheim, Ramillies, Oudenarde and Malplaquet, Mary was the granddaughter of the 5th Earl Cadogan, whose family had inherited the ever-increasingly lucrative Manor of Chelsea from the Sloanes. Her father, Lord Chelsea, had died young and her mother, a Sturt (from the same West Country dynasty, incidentally, as the husband cuckolded by the 5th Duke of Marlborough), later remarried first a Lambton and then a Montagu. Immensely capable, practical and determined (her jaw says it all), Mary proved a sterling wife to Bert and a veritable eighth tower at Blenheim. It is noticeable that all the old retainers around the estate use the same expressions to describe their former mistress, whom they clearly regarded with a mixture of awe, respect and admiration: "a real Duchess" and "a true lady".

Chips Channon, an old Oxford friend of Ivor's, who characteristically claimed to have spent much of his youth "under the old regime" was also impressed by Mary's healthy influence on Blenheim. On his first visit in her time as *châtelaine*, he noted in his diary:

> Mary Marlborough has improved the house and has enhanced the atmosphere. It is now gay and healthy, and the long corridors echo with childish laughter and screams, and huge dogs sprawl about. In the evenings, the fantastic terraces and gardens are floodlighted (I think that all gardens should be floodlit now, it is a wonderful invention and the effect is fantastic, rich and beautiful). On Sunday I was next to Mary Marlborough at luncheon, and got to like her quite enormously. She is an efficient Duchess, handsome, gay, and serious-minded, very English, very balanced, very conventional and brings up her children in a rather snappy, almost Spartan simple way: and they seem to adore her.

Bert and Mary had five children: two sons (Sunny, the present Duke, born in 1926, and an "afterthought", Charles, born in 1940) and three daughters (Sarah, Caroline and Rosemary). "When we moved into Blenheim in 1934," recalls the present Duke, "we used to ride in the grounds and we also had a game of bicycle-tag riding around the cellar passageways . . . I cannot recall any horrible accidents." Ted Wadman, the 10th Duke's long-serving butler, remembers the younger children riding through the staff's legs in the basement quarters. Sunny's

Duchess Mary at Blenheim with three of her granddaughters: Alexandra, Serena and Mimi Russell.

schoolfriends who came to stay joined in the fun; on one occasion Wadman gave Ian Gilmour, the future politician, a clout around the ear. Paul Maze, the artist who did several paintings of Blenheim, presented the young Marquess of Blandford with a splendid collection of lead soldiers which are now on display in the Great Hall.

Children enjoying themselves brought a welcome touch of humanity to Blenheim. In Sunny's day, as Phon Hollis recalls, there was no bicycling allowed in the park or walking on the grass, cameras were confiscated and the gardeners were supposed to down tools and "disappear" when a member of the

Hunting days in Leicestershire. The present Duke with his sisters, Lady Sarah (left) and Lady Caroline, join their father (background, examining his hat) at a meet.

family or a guest hove into view. The new Duke, a practical gardener, stopped the latter nonsense, liking to see his employees at work about the place. Tom Page, who later became Head Gardener, came down with the Duke and Duchess from Lowesby, together with the stock plants. His first job at Blenheim was to be foreman of the Greenhouse department of over half a dozen men; Phon Hollis was foreman of the Pleasure Grounds with a further eight men while the Kitchen Garden brought the total number of those working on the gardens up to about thirty. The number was not to decrease significantly until the 1960s.

In addition to supplying such favourite plants and flowers for the house as hybrid begonias (shooting season), delphiniums, white peonies and carnations (for Ascot), the gardeners had to produce vegetables (the Duke being particularly partial to peas, broad beans and spinach) and a cornucopia of hothouse fruit – melons, grapes, both Muscat and Madresfield, peaches, nectarines and, especially, figs – plus strawberries and raspberries. The pay for the gardeners, which rose to about 26s. plus accommodation, before the Second World War, was considered well above average. Members of the public were admitted on conducted tours of the garden for 6*d*.

Indoors, the staff wages ranged from about £5 per week for the French chef to under £1 a week for junior housemaids and laundrymaids. When Ted Wadman, later the Duke's butler and confidant, arrived at Blenheim in 1938 as under-butler he was on 30*s*. a week. The establishment was pretty much as it had been in Consuelo's day at the turn of the century: butler, under-butler, groom of the chambers, three or four footmen, two "odd" men; housekeeper and half-a-dozen housemaids, two still-room maids; the chef and perhaps another half-a-dozen in the kitchen. The still-liveried footmen's duties included swinging scent, contained in long rods, around the rooms; the electric bulbs were also fitted with scent-filled asbestos rings. The Duke and Duchess tended to eat formally in the Saloon, semi-formally in the Bow Window Room and less formally sometimes in the restored Indian Room of the 5th Duke, down by the water terraces to the west. Coffee, liqueurs and the "grog tray" would be placed in the Long Library. The butler, whom the junior servants called "Sir", would himself dine (black tie, etc.) in what was known as the "Pugs Parlour" together with the Duke's valet and the head housekeeper, while the under-butler would preside over meals in the Servants' Hall for the rest of the staff. Wadman says that they did themselves fairly well with joints of meat, though the beer did not always flow so freely as some would have wished. "When I said to my boss, the butler (Mr Taylor, a man of about 18 stone), that I was thirsty after some exhausting job or other, he replied: 'Hedward my boy, there is plenty of water in the tap.'"

In the late 1930s Bert and Mary entertained on a princely scale. Such aristocratic names as Curzon, Londonderry, Weymouth, Montagu, Dudley, Carnarvon and Grosvenor recur frequently in the Visitors' Book. The Kents and the Gloucesters were among the royal guests and the most celebrated visit of the immediate prewar period was in June 1936 when the reigning King Edward VIII came to stay in a house party that included the Duke and Duchess of Buccleuch, Duff and Diana Cooper, the Winston Churchills and the American hostess Lady ("Emerald") Cunard. Among the other guests were a Mr and Mrs Ernest Simpson.

That autumn the Marlboroughs were among those staying up at Balmoral when the King shocked the Scots by picking up Mrs Simpson from Aberdeen Station, having earlier refused an invitation to open new hospital buildings in that city. Edward and Mrs Simpson's friend, Herman Rogers, made a home-movie about this controversial house party which he ran at the gathering after the Windsors' wedding; among the audience was Cecil Beaton, who noted in his diary that Mary Marlborough was not "flattered by the camera". Bert was described by Beaton on another occasion as having a "silly baby face, arrogant stare and bad manners".

During the Abdication crisis that other acute twentieth-century diarist, Chips Channon, had seen Mary Marlborough at a party given by Emerald Cunard. The Duchess, wrote Chips

> asked me in her frank breezy way, did I not think that all the while Wallis had been playing a double game? She herself has not yet made up her mind, but she added that it enraged her when people attacked Emerald for entertaining her, as Emerald was only one of many. "We had her to stay at Blenheim, I liked her," was Mary's summing up.

The undoubted high spot of Bert and Mary's early years at Blenheim was the coming-out ball for their eldest daughter, Lady Sarah Spencer-Churchill in July 1939. "It was the most elaborate party I ever planned," the Duchess told *Woman's Journal* after the war. "The organization required for coping with a thousand guests was tremendous." The whole palace was gloriously floodlit, with Japanese lanterns and chains of coloured lights hung around the terraces and searchlights playing in the trees. "Before the ball," recalled the Duchess, "we held a private dinner party in the Saloon, and Sarah had another one for some of the younger guests on the terrace facing the lake. Trees, six feet high, surrounded the dinner table, and lights shining through orange awnings, high up on the terraces gave an effect like sunlight." Tom Page remembers helping to put hundreds of white lilies in place among the decorations. The orchestra played Viennese waltzes in the Long Library.

The guests included the Duke of Kent, the American Ambassador's daughter Eunice Kennedy, sister of the ill-fated President, and Lady Sarah's grandmother, Consuelo Balsan, who supped with Winston Churchill and Anthony Eden. "In this brilliant scene at Blenheim," wrote Consuelo in *The Glitter and the Gold*, "I sensed the end of an era."

Lady Sarah's ball came to symbolize the last bright summer of peace. In her autobiography *Mercury Presides* Daphne Fielding says it put her in mind of the ball given by the Duchess of Richmond on the eve of Waterloo. Chips Channon recorded the "stupendous" event in his diary:

> I have seen much, travelled far and am accustomed to splendour, but there has never been anything like tonight. Tyroleans walked about singing; and although there were seven hundred people or even more, it was not in the least crowded. It was gay, young, brilliant, in short, perfection. I was loath to leave, but did so at about 4.30 and took one last look at the baroque terraces with the lake below, and the golden statues and the great palace. Shall we ever see the like again? Is such a function not out of date? Yet it was all of the England that is supposed to be dead and is not.

Above all, this sublime moment in Blenheim's history was immortalized by Sir Sacheverell Sitwell:

> The whole of Blenheim was floodlit for the ball, from panoramic court and scenic portico to the dark cedars on the lawn and the bust of "Le Roi Soleil", a prisoner, upon the pediment; from the powdered hair and "Padua" scarlet of the state liveries, through the crowded ballrooms, down to the room hung with "Indian" papers that look out upon Bernini's fountain; to the shelves of water and the deep lake that seemed to move and flow. There was a galaxy of light upon this theatrical, but heroic building, upon this private monument that is a Roman triumph and a public pantomime; and amid those lights it was possible to admire Vanbrugh's architecture as it may never be seen again.

Soon Blenheim was being blacked out for the Second World War ("quite a task," as the Duchess said, with "more than a thousand windows"). "After all the trouble we took," recalled the Duchess, "refurbishing the palace, getting new curtains for many of the rooms, giving the whole place a face-lift . . . ", life for the Marlboroughs was suddenly irrevocably changed. Despite the carnage of the "Great War", life at home had gone on pretty much as before, but 1939 marked a point of no return for the old world.

In the First World War the Long Library had been pressed into service as a hospital for wounded servicemen. In the Second, 400 boys from Malvern College were evacuated, at the Duke's suggestion, to Blenheim and stayed for a year before moving on to Harrow-on-the-Hill. The Long Library became an overcrowded dormitory, the Great Hall a dining-room and the whole house and its out-buildings were turned upside down under matting and linoleum. Hideous utility huts littered the Great Court; shatter-tape criss-crossed the windows.

Malvern was followed by no less a body than MI5, the intelligence service which had moved down from its former quarters in Wormwood Scrubs. The hush-hush nature of the mysterious "government department" employing up to a thousand people was not a very well-kept secret. Apparently bus conductors used to call out at the gates of Blenheim: "Anyone for MI5?" Later temporary residents at Blenheim in wartime included members of the British Council and the Ministry of Supply. Meanwhile, the Marlboroughs had retreated to the privacy of the east wing. Although the State Rooms were fully redecorated after the war, never again were they to be used on an "everyday" basis as they had been in the past.

Bert, who had retired as a Captain in the Life Guards a dozen years earlier, rejoined the army and served as Military Liaison Officer to the Southern Region Commander. He also put his American connections to good use as a Lieutenant-Colonel

Opposite: Not a job that can be delegated. Duchess Mary dusts the china.

The Long Library doubling as a dormitory and classroom for the evacuated boys of Malvern College, 1939.

liaising with the United States Forces. During the early part of the war his wife rather outranked him, being Chief Commandant of the ATS. Bert called Mary "the General".

The Countess of Drogheda told a wartime anecdote of how a visiting Polish General was sitting next to a handsome English General who spoke in a deep voice about strategy. Suddenly, to the Pole's astonishment, the English General took out a powder puff, then a lipstick. It was the Duchess of Marlborough.

The Duchess, who stood no nonsense, had a remarkable knack of getting things done whether at Blenheim or in the bureaucratic jungle of war. When the ATS were short of typewriters she drove direct to the War Office and refused to leave until they put some machines in the back of her car. In 1940 after the birth of her young son Charles (described by Chips Channon in 1945 as "a very pretty petulant, sophisticated Hoppner of a child"), the Duchess relinquished her command in the ATS and took on the Presidency of the Oxfordshire Red Cross (driving thousands of miles organizing the rural "Penny Collections"), as well as working tirelessly for the WVS. Both the Duke and Duchess helped raise money for many worthy wartime causes; during an open-air sale in Woodstock's War Weapons week, Bert shared

Landing craft practising at Blenheim during the Second World War.

the role of auctioneer with the comedian Gillie Potter. An autographed photograph of Bert's cousin Winston, now enjoying his finest hour as the Churchillian saviour of the beleagured nation, fetched £250. In 1942 the Duke obtained permission from the Food Minister, Lord Woolton, for the tench, perch, pike and eels to be caught from the lake and sold in the shops. The gardens were converted to full-scale food production, as they had been in the First World War.

As the Duke said later of Blenheim in the war years, "altogether it was a very different affair from an historic house". But at least the Spencer-Churchills were together for most of the time. Lady Sarah (alias "Miss Churchill") worked as a machinist in the Morris Motors factory at Cowley under the foremanship of one of the Blenheim servants. "I don't suppose I have ever had a stranger-looking staff than the constantly changing odd job men we had then," said the Duchess. "The whole family had to help with the work, and eating was like a continual picnic."

After the war the Ministry of Works lent a hand in the long process of rehabilitation. The palace had to have new paint, new gilt, new floors, almost new everything. The days of heating the whole house with a ton of coal every twenty-four hours would

The schoolboys of Malvern College in the Great Court.

never return. Noel Coward, who brightened the postwar gloom at Blenheim with his private piano recitals to Princess Margaret and the *jeunesse dorée* of the time, found his bedroom

> the coldest room I have ever encountered . . . Woke frozen. Shaving sheer agony and glacial bathroom with a skylight that would not shut. Loo like an icebox. Breakfast downstairs. Bert Marlborough none too bright – Mary very sweet. Saw Princess Margaret off. Pretended I was going to Oxford but actually drove back to Notley [then the seat of Sir Laurence Olivier] where I had lunch and played canasta. Returned to Blenheim at cocktail time. Small dinner. More piano playing. Back to the Frigidaire. Lit the gas fire like Peggy Ashcroft [in the suicide scene in Terence Rattigan's *The Deep Blue Sea*] and burrowed into bed in socks and a sweater.

Princess Margaret was a frequent visitor to Blenheim and at one time her name was inevitably linked with the Marlboroughs' son and heir, Lord Blandford. In the 1950s the Princess was twice guest of honour at the Dior Fashion Shows presented at the palace in aid of the Red Cross. The young Yves St Laurent's finale for the second show was a creation called "Blenheim", an evening dress of white satin, its long sleeves a thoughtful acknowledgement of the draughty corridors in English country houses.

Opposite: Bert and Princess Margaret at the Blenheim Garden Party for the Coronation summer of 1953.

At Blenheim in the postwar period the shortage of servants, often regarded as one of the causes of the dissolution of the country house, was only relative. There was still a hard core of middle-aged retainers who had worked there since prewar years and these stalwarts were supplemented by foreigners who, in the days before Continental Europe had outstripped Britain in prosperity, were easy to come by. When Ted Wadman returned to take up the job of butler in 1947 (at £8 per week) he still had four footmen, mostly Italians. As the New Elizabethan Age dawned and Winston Churchill returned to power, the aristocracy experienced a period of recovery such as nobody could have envisaged amidst the privations of the Second World War and its austere socialist aftermath. Even so uncompromising a pessimist as Evelyn Waugh had to admit in 1959 that his evocation of the past glories of aristocratic life in *Brideshead Revisited*, written fifteen years earlier, was "a panegyric preached over an empty coffin".

The main feature of postwar life at Blenheim was the palace and grounds being thrown open on a scale never attempted before the war. In April 1950 the coroneted key to the lock of the entrance door (a lock copied from the gates of Warsaw) turned to admit the first flush of visitors at a half-crown a head. Despite indifferent weather 230 people rolled up on the first day and soon the figures were reaching the thousands. One eager tripper dumped her newborn baby with the Duchess while she joined a conducted tour. Members of the Spencer-Churchill family were pressed into service and stray guests such as Bert's shooting crony, "Porchey" Carnarvon, found themselves acting as temporary guides. David Green's masterly guide book (a condensed version of his *magnum opus* on the palace which was to be published in 1951) sold briskly at another half-crown under the salesmanship of Lady Rosemary Spencer-Churchill. Garden produce, trinkets, souvenirs, car park fees, and so forth, brought in the cash. "All this is very necessary," the Duke told the *Daily Mirror*. "Without these half-crown entrance fees we couldn't possibly keep the place going. Taxation, y'know. Crippling."

In 1951 Blenheim topped the new "stately home" charts, beating Lord Bath's then still lionless Longleat into second place. Under the capable management of the Glaswegian Archie ("Jock") Illingworth, Head Guide from 1953 to 1972, the initially amateurish operation, started in the early days of such enterprises, developed into a smoothly organized piece of showmanship. "Our record day saw 6,300 visitors come to the palace," recalls Jock. "1,200 of them arrived in the first hour and they were queuing up right round the Great Court." Illingworth worked out a flow system to speed the filter through the State Rooms which has since been refined by his successor, Paul Duffie.

In Illingworth's experience, French schoolchildren are the worst behaved; he once came across a group of them trying to

Opposite: Princess Margaret at the Dior Dress Show at Blenheim, 1952. Lady Caroline Waterhouse and the present Duke are seated to the Princess's right.

kick down a door and threw them out. He also had to eject an obstreperous Conservative Member of Parliament and his friend when they barged their way into the palace after closing time. An ugly row ensued, with the police being called and the MP contemptuously referring to Illingworth as "that lout", but the Duke characteristically backed up his Head Guide in his actions. The MP, incidentally, was also later turned out by his constituents.

Bert, a television addict, liked to be told if any celebrities or "VIPs" turned up. During the filming of *Half-a-Sixpence* (adapted from a novel of another sometime Blenheim gate-crasher, H.G. Wells) there was the improbable combination to be seen in Sir Winston Churchill's Birth Room of the film's star, Tommy Steele, and Robert Kennedy, the President's equally ill-fated brother. On another occasion, Illingworth received a message from the Savoy Hotel in London that King Umberto of Italy wanted to come down to see Blenheim. He duly informed the Duke. "Should I have him for lunch?" mused Bert. On learning from his current shooting guest, the Duke of Windsor, who arrived with a black valet in tow, that Umberto (or "Beppo" as he was known) was "a damn nice feller", Bert decided to offer the exiled monarch the run of his table and cellar. "Bring him along then, what?" he told Illingworth.

Sir Winston, as he became in 1954 (accepting the Garter but turning down a dukedom of his own), continued to be a regular visitor under the new regime. During his years in opposition he spoke at a major political rally on the south lawn and in Coronation Year, as Prime Minister, he was among the guests at the Blenheim Garden Party, attended by Princess Margaret. Colourful figures from the Commonwealth dressed in national costume cheered up the rather dull day – not least the beaming Oceanic Queen, Selote of Tonga, who had recently stolen the show in the Coronation procession, while the band of Bert's old regiment, the Life Guards, oompahed nostalgically away.

Blenheim was also among the early stately homes to catch on to the fact that it is not visitors through the gate that help pay the bills so much as special events and "functions". In Bert's day these ranged from rallies in the park by the Pony Club, guild of Lady Drivers and Rolls-Royce owners, to water-ski shows on the lake and other diversions. A miniature railway was constructed in the Lower Park; Bert, a model train enthusiast, also had his own toy tracks put up in the Orangery. In 1969 Princess Alexandra attended the première of the *Son et Lumière* performance on the south front of Blenheim which Sunny Blandford had set up in aid of the Red Cross. Richard Burton's voice doubled as the two national heroes in the story – the 1st Duke and Sir Winston – and his then wife Elizabeth Taylor was among the audience. The event, in the end, proved only a qualified success. The original idea had been to have the show on the entrance front but Bert, with his usual directness, had pointed out the problem of seating

the audience on the far side of the lake. They would, Bert claimed, find themselves sitting on cowpats.

Bert kept what he called "a watchful eye" on the park and, towards the end of his life, was taking an interest in the prospects of barley-fed cattle ("I can't say I like the taste of barley-fed beef myself, but it seems very popular"). But shooting always took precedence over agriculture, as Bill Murdock, the Duke's agent from 1953 onwards, recalls. "He wouldn't have sheep in the park," says the genial Murdock. "Said they made too much bloody mess and ate all his cover." The keepers ruled the roost in Bert's day and the estate was run on a benevolent "live and let live" basis. "Somehow we managed to balance the books," says Murdock who retired to a house in Bladon, just nearby Ted Wadman, the former butler, in 1978.

"The Duke was one of the great shots of our time," says Bill Murdock. "He had a perfect style; never hurried." Sometimes the Duke would potter into the estate office and ask Murdock: "What are you doing this afternoon? Let's shoot a few cocks, what?" Regular guns in the shooting parties at Blenheim included Lord Carnarvon and his son Lord Porchester; Lord Cadogan; Antony Lambton, the politician and writer; and

Tommy Steele shows Robert Kennedy Sir Winston Churchill's Birth Room during a break in the filming of Half a Sixpence *at Blenheim, 1967. Archie Illingworth, the Head Guide, is between them. Bert is on the left of the picture, glass in hand.*

Bert and Sir Winston Churchill during the 1953 Blenheim Garden Party.

Opposite: Sir Winston with Duchess Mary at Blenheim.

Jeremy Tree, the racing trainer. "Porchey" Carnarvon and Bert would wage a constant war of mutual teasing; one of the former's running jokes was that the food at Blenheim was not up to scratch ("Bert, this bloody salmon isn't cooked!", etc.). When out shooting with David Niven, Bert brought down a carrier pigeon. "See if there are any messages for me, will you Bert?" asked the actor, who claimed it took the Duke a week to see the joke.

As well as being a favourite butt in shooting stories, Bert was also supposed to have been the author of many outrageous remarks that belong to aristocratic folklore. "The trouble with you," he once addressed a fellow peer, "is that you're not one of us." After a lavish shooting lunch at Stype, Sir Charles Clore's place near Hungerford, Bert muttered: "Extraordinary chap, Clore. Gave us goose. No gentleman gives goose to his guests these days, what?" As for Paul Getty, when it was pointed out to Bert by Wadman that the Duke's regular Monday treat of cottage

Shooting party at Blenheim, 1953; Bert in his element.

pie might be a little "ordinary" for the multi-millionaire, Bert barked out: "What about it? Mr Getty is a very *ordinary* little man, isn't he?" When an American lady lit up a cigarette in the middle of dinner at Blenheim one night, Bert asked what she thought she was doing. She said that she liked smoking between courses. Bert proceeded to tell her that he liked doing a number of things – one of which he spelt out in his most uncompromising manner – but that he didn't do it between course at mealtimes.

One of the best-known items in the Bert Marlborough mythology can be found wrapped up in Alastair Forbes's inimitable prose in the following extract from one of his witty stream of snobbery reviews in the *Spectator*:

When the late President Jack Kennedy's sister-in-law, Lee Bouvier Radziwill sometime Canfield, was trying to find a bottom rung to hoist herself out of café and into High Society, she went for the weekend to Blenheim, more of a snake than a ladder one would have thought in that struggle for survival. I asked her had she got on with the Duke (his present Grace's graceless father, "Bert"). "Oh, it was fine", she said. "Only the Duke 'went to the bathroom in the fireplace.'" I could only sigh, "Will you never learn English."

Another American guest at Blenheim is said to have asked politely if he might try one of the Duke's cigars. Bert is supposed to have come back with: "They don't grow on trees y'know."

In Bert's time there was no "dedication" plan for woodland, though some 350 acres of woods were planted. The Blenheim woods were looked after by a remarkable quintet, Messrs Slatter, Pike, Parsons, Townsend and Stockford, who worked together in harness for over forty years right up to the 1960s. Rather resembling *The Little Gren Men* of the forest, they happily beavered away in an ancient rural ritual of their own. "It was a good outdoor life," recalls the spry Harry Stockford, the pensioner on the Blenheim estate with the longest service to his credit. Brought up at Bladon, he began work on the Blenheim woods in 1925 (52 hours a week in the summer months, 48 in the winter) and retired in 1981. For their breaks in the winter the woodmen would huddle around a fire they lit in the open air. "The work was interesting; everyone was friendly; you were free as a bird and I enjoyed it." Part of the woodmen's work was to act as beaters for the shoot. "The 10th Duke lived for his shooting," recalls Stockford. Other guns he particularly remembers are Duff Cooper and the late Duke of Kent.

Bert never tired of the whiskered old jokes about his "private parts" at Blenheim or how he was supposed to have "the biggest private organ in the country". Someone staying at Blenheim in the early 1960s remembers Bert buttonholing him: "I will show you my private parts – you know, what, where the public aren't allowed. They're rather pretty my private parts and they have got a lot of colour." Bert's genuine love and knowledge of botany could surprise and touch those who had previously written him off as a pompous boor. A mistake often made in generalizing about the aristocracy is to assume that because they wear tweeds, understand estate management, like sport and country pursuits, they must be moronic philistines. Whereas they might well also have absorbed more about art, architecture and the rest through, so to speak, having been brought up with them, than many a clever specialist in those subjects.

Prodding a lily with his stick as he conducted a guest around his newly created garden to the south-east of the palace with modest pride, Bert would say: "We've transplanted a lot of stuff from the woods to get this to grow. Now – this Ruhimia I transferred has a very pretty habit."

The 10th Duke's garden, which is indeed protected by "PRIVATE notices, was not begun until 1954. It came about as the result of Bert receiving a legacy. The wild, romantic garden was essentially English though influenced by eighteenth-century Italian gardens. Where there was formerly rough grass there is now a secret labyrinth of ponds, stones (transported from Gladys's old Rock Garden by the Great Cascade) and a network of paths. He worked on it for the rest of his life, his special

Above: Bert takes a dip in the water terraces.
Left: Lady Rosemary Spencer-Churchill and her husband, Robin Muir.
Below: Ted Wadman, the butler, instructs the footmen on the finer points of cleaning silver

Above: Four generations in a family group at Blenheim. Back row (left to right): Lord Charles Spencer-Churchill, Robin Muir, Hugo Waterhouse, Bert, Lord Blandford (now the present Duke) and Ed Russell. Middle row: Duchess Mary, Lady Caroline Waterhouse (with David Waterhouse), Lady Ivor Spencer-Churchill, Mme Jacques Balsan (Bert's mother, Consuelo), Lady Blandford (Susan with her son James, then styled Earl of Sunderland), and Lady Rosemary Muir. Front row: Elizabeth Waterhouse, Robert Spencer-Churchill (Lord Ivor's son), Alexander Muir and Michael Waterhouse.

Dinner party at Blenheim in the Bow Window Room.

Left: All in a day's work.
Above: Clearing the lake.
Below: The chandeliers and clocks.
Right: Two Blenheim stalwarts:
Tom Jakeman, the long-serving
boilerman (above) and the now
retired Head Gardener, Tom Page,
with a new strain of orchid which
he developed at Blenheim (below).

assistant being Bob Deacon. "When His Grace used to come back from London," recalls Deacon, "he would leap out of the car and head straight for his garden, arriving there even before his standard could be raised at Flagstaff Lodge to announce his return." Deacon would often be summoned from his cottage at weekends to satisfy the botanical curiosity of the Duke's guests. A disciplinarian of the old school, Deacon always used to be smartly turned out in a collar and tie, polished boots, a cap (frequently doffed) covering his neatly-cropped hair ("No long-haired poets in the gardens").

While Bert pottered about his beloved garden or chatted with a familiar face about the estate (an essentially shy man, he did not like to see strangers at Blenheim), Mary ran the palace with consummate authority. "The Duchess was very appreciative of work well done," recalls Sid Jakeman who took over the boilers from his legendary father Tom in the early 1950s and was also in charge of plumbing and the waterworks. Jack Hirst, an electrical engineer who became general foreman at Blenheim, always found the Duchess straightforward and fair; they would work together preparing the table decoration for the Christmas dinner in the Saloon. "The Duchess always wanted something topical constructed for the occasion," recalls the ingenious Hirst. "One year I made a Russian sputnik using a disguised tennis ball wired to rotate around a globe. Another year, after one of the Dior shows, we devised a fashion parade with dolls." Sadly, Duchess Mary never saw Hirst's most ambitious creation, a model of Vanbrugh's bridge across the lake which he made for Christmas 1960. She was too ill, dying of cancer a few months later. One of the old retainers recalls seeing a wreath at the Duchess's funeral from her doctor inscribed: "To the bravest lady I know."

At Blenheim the 1960s were a melancholy period. The constant restoration of the palace continued ("During the past ten years I've spent £60,000 of my own money on the stone-work alone," said the 10th Duke in 1969, "and the government has spent an equal amount") but after Mary's death the atmosphere was lacking in love. There was the occasional event – such as the delayed 21st birthday party for Lord Charles Spencer-Churchill combined with a coming-out party for his niece Serena Russell – when the old spark returned, but guests on the private side found Blenheim increasingly solemn.

Bert hoped to marry again. His old friend Laura Charteris (then the widow of American publisher Michael Canfield, said to be an illegitimate son of the Duke of Kent, and previously the wife of the 3rd Earl of Dudley and of the 2nd Viscount Long) recalled in her lively memoirs, *Laughter from a Cloud:*

> I was fond of him but, as I frequently explained, Blenheim was so terribly gloomy. It was built as a monument, not a house to

live in. At times Bert would try to counter this statement by quoting the many thousands of paying tourists who flocked to Blenheim each year. But he did not see that this made it even worse than gloomy by turning him and his friends into exhibits, like freaks or animals to be gazed at. I felt this most acutely when playing croquet in the public eye, surrounded by a chain to keep the not unnaturally inquisitive visitors off the lawn. I thought at any moment they would throw us stale bread or nuts as in the zoo . . .

Secretly, I believe, Bert was in agreement with me. His reason for continuing to inhabit Blenheim – or as he came (through me) to call it, "the Dump" – was a real fear of being the first Duke not to reside there. For despite being a wonderful example of workmanship, it was a mausoleum.

By Christmas 1971, however, Laura had changed her mind about taking on Bert and Blenheim. Describing the dinner on Christmas night for Bert's family she had to admit that Blenheim

now appeared magnificent in an historical way. At dinner two large fires blazed with yule logs; it really was "glitter and gold". The vast table was heaped with a sumptuous feast of

Bert with his elder son and new daughter-in-law, Athina Livanos (Tina Onassis).

highly decorated cold food, boar's head, pheasants with their tail feathers like flags to call attention to their poor aspic-covered bodies, lobsters with their red claws in abundance amongst this culinary display. The dinner plates were golden colour, in reality silver gilt. The chairs were large and comfortable, if cumbersome, but at least suitably regal in appearance for a festive Christmas dinner. I was seated opposite Bert. This was the way, he insisted, the *"place à table"* should be whenever I visited Blenheim. Now it mattered no longer, for it was common knowledge that we were to marry.

Bert and Laura were married at Caxton Hall in the New Year. At the luncheon afterwards at the Connaught (cooked by the former chef at Blenheim, whose parting gift to the Duke was the detailed icing-sugar model of the palace now on display in the Long Library), Bert rose to his feet. Fixing his eyes on Laura, he movingly attempted to sing one of his favourite old music hall songs: "I shan't be happy till I make her happy too". Three months later he was dead.

Deputizing for Bert at the staff party which he was too ill to attend after their wedding, the new Duchess told them that they should bring their problems to her in person and she would always do her best to sort out any troubles they might have; that as yet she only knew a few people in this crowded place but before long she would know everyone individually. Sadly, it was not to be.

Bert was buried at Bladon, next to his first wife Mary, and not far from where Sir Winston Churchill lies. The 10th Duke was borne to his grave by some of his senior staff. He is remembered with affection, humour and understanding by many of those who worked for him at Blenheim. They knew his rages were only temporary. "He would swear at his workers," says Bob Deacon, "but they would merely swear back at him. He was then apt to stamp off and forget all about it."

Bert's dealings with his staff exemplified the mutual respect that is the hallmark of the old aristocrat-servant relationship – a point often missed by modern actors and actresses who portray aristocrats as either too haughty or too familiar and servants as either resentful or fawning. Bert enjoyed a striking rapport with his butler Ted Wadman and carried on a constant cross-talk act with his erratic valet-cum-chauffeur, the late Freddie Bramwell. Driving the Duke back from the Royal Meeting at Ascot, Bramwell had had a few drinks too many (not an unusual event). The Duke kept looking at Bramwell out of the corner of his eye and the chauffeur kept looking out of the corner of his eye to see if he were being watched by his employer. Not surprisingly they missed the right road home, taking two-and-a-half hours to do an hour's journey. When they finally reached the palace, Bert was heard giving Bramwell some stick:

"You know I'm a magistrate and could sentence you to five years' imprisonment for being in charge while under the influence of drink."

"Oh, you wouldn't do that to me, Your Grace."

"By jove, I would. This is becoming an annual occurrence."

"But I only had two glasses of vin rosy."

"*Vin Rosé*? Beer's your drink, man!"

On another notorious occasion Bramwell's state of inebriation at the wheel so infuriated the Duke that he ordered him to stop the car. He then dragged the chauffeur from the front seat, deposited him on the kerbside and drove himself to London. Much to his surprise the door of his house in Shepherd's Place was opened by a perfectly sober Bramwell. How he managed this remains one of Blenheim's much-discussed mysteries.

Bert's name lives on in a hundred anecdotes. Many of them turn on his remoteness from the modern world. There is the old chestnut about his asking one of his daughters why his toothbrush was not foaming properly; it having not occurred to him that one had to apply toothpaste, something usually done by his then absent valet. When he found himself having to make conversation with two policemen who had called at Blenheim, a topic eluded him until he remembered his beloved television.

"You really must see Dixon of Dock Green," he told them amiably. "First class programme, y'know. All about you fellers."

Jack Hirst recalls how mystified he was by the practicalities of life. "Why isn't my radiator working, Hirst?" the Duke asked him during a power cut. The engineer attempted to explain. "But my fire is working all right," said the Duke.

The following dialogue took place at Blenheim in the 1960s between Bert and a youngish aristocratic lady living alone in the country.

"You've got no servants?"

"I look after myself."

"But not all by yourself, surely?"

"I have a woman to come in in the mornings to clean for a bit but I have no cook."

"No cook? How extraordinary, then who does the cooking?"

"I do."

"But do you mean to say you know how to cook?"

"Yes, I cook very well."

"But why did you learn?"

"Well I had to."

"But you mean to say that when you have people for the weekend you cook for them?"

"Well I don't like to spend all my time in the kitchen when friends are there so I do all my cooking for the weekend on a Thursday."

"On Thursday? How extraordinary. How do the things keep all that time?"

"Well, I cooked things like egg mousses that do keep."

"Egg mousses, huh, and can you cook proper things? Can you cook a *terrine de Gitier*?"

"Yes I can do a terrine."

"This is the most extraordinary thing I have ever heard."

As a friend (believed to be Antony Lambton) wrote to *The Times* after Bert's death, the late Duke of Marlborough was "Like nobody else":

Over six foot tall, with a splendid if somewhat petulant appearance, he seemed in scale to the great Palace and Park at Blenheim to which he devoted the latter half of his life. There he lived the life of a nineteenth-century country gentleman – shooting (he was a magnificent shot), gardening and following with fascination the vagaries of British weather: he went his way. Times changed, he did not. The type he personified is easy to criticize, yet to dismiss him easily would be to sacrifice character to mundane convention as he had two rare qualities – wit and an appreciation of wit. These, allied to his conservatism, may have made him appear formidable and to strangers frightening, but behind the mumbling and the muttering, the malacca cane, the gold watch chain and seals lay a kind heart

and he was greatly loved by his children and grandchildren while to his friends he was a source of endless pleasure.

But above all he was a personality remaining himself, sometimes to be laughed at, more often to be laughed with, but never to go unnoticed. In these grey days he will be sadly missed.

Bert and friends playing croquet on the lawn, the east front (with its private apartments) in the background. Another Patrick Lichfield photograph taken for Life *in the 1960s.*

7. The present Battle for Blenheim

"And where in the park did the battle take place?" This old chestnut remains one of the perennially popular questions asked by the less knowledgeable visitors to Blenheim Palace. The 10th Duke of Marlborough could not resist telling the endearingly gullible hostess, Laura Corrigan (social-climbing daughter of a lumberjack from Cleveland, Ohio) that the column in the park marked the exact spot. The present Duke tends to turn the question on its head by describing his campaign to maintain, restore and preserve the palace as his own "never-ending Battle of Blenheim".

If under his father Blenheim could be said to have been remarkably feudal, today it is fundamentally a commercial operation, geared to economic survival. "Blenheim is very much a business now," the Duke says. "Our turnover is well over £2 million and it has more than doubled in the last ten years; all the money is simply ploughed back into keeping Blenheim going." The palace is now open every day between March and October (in 1984 361,547 people toured the inside); the estate runs to some 11,500 acres (of which nearly a third is farmed "in hand" by the Duke); and during the summer up to 180 people are employed in some capacity at Blenheim, with about half of these working all the year round. The business is tidily divided up into different departments (farms, palace administration, forestry, gardens, game, stud, gift shops, private wing), each managed by its own executive head, with Paul Hutton, the agent, in a role analogous to that of managing director and with the 11th Duke as a beady-eyed chairman, wired for sound in his car ("Number 11" is, appropriately enough, his call-sign) and armed, even when riding, with a portable dictaphone.

The arrival of Blenheim into the modern world was not, however, a crash landing made in 1972 upon the death of the 10th Duke. His heir had already received substantial parts of the estate by way of marriage settlements and, at least on paper, had been the effective owner of most of the property since the early 1960s – even if, out of respect for his father in residence, he felt obliged to make changes somewhat cautiously. The 10th Duke's transfer of the assets in his lifetime helped reduce the capital taxation which otherwise could have taken as much as four-fifths of the family fortunes and thereby have effectively ended the Spencer-Churchills' connexion with Blenheim. In the event, the 11th Duke was able to meet the death duty tax bill without selling

Opposite: The present Duke and Duchess.

either works of art or land but by offering about 30,000 documents from the Marlborough Papers at Blenheim to the Treasury (they are now in the British Museum). "As these documents were already available for study," he said at the time, "one thought that their transfer to the British Museum would not be any loss to the estate or family."

As this remark might imply, the Duke is not a scholar or a bookworm but an essentially practical man. Like several Churchills, he may not have shone academically at school, but the Duke of Marlborough has turned out to be nobody's fool. Behind the apparently austere manner and somewhat inscrutable expression, with the piercingly Churchillian blue eyes, there operates a shrewd brain that knows exactly what is required and how to achieve it. "When you think you've done all you can," says the palace administrator Paul Duffie, "he'll pick up the one thing you've missed." Duffie, a former Warrant Officer in the Scots Guards, adds, "I've known commanding officers like that."

The military allusion is very apt, for the Duke readily admits that he does run Blenheim rather in the manner of a regiment with himself as CO. His own time in the army emphatically shaped his personality and he speaks of his military experiences with an engaging warmth. He joined up straight from Eton in 1944, serving in the ranks of the Life Guards for the last six months of the Second World War before receiving a commission.

An extremely shy person, and always rather young for his years (he was born in 1926), the Duke found that the army gave him a much-needed boost of self-confidence: "It helped me to get on better with other people." He liked the discipline and enjoyed the responsibility of looking after his troops under canvas and elsewhere. During his nine years in the army he served in Germany and Egypt as well as doing stints of Household Cavalry duty in London. Life in the "Tins" was clearly congenial and he savoured the contrast between the pageantry of the traditional ceremonies like Trooping the Colour and the modern mechanical element of the armoured cars. He was on parade at King George VI's funeral in 1952 and in 1953 at the Coronation of the present Queen (who is, incidentally, almost his exact contemporary, being just thirteen days older than the Duke) before he retired from the Life Guards, as a Captain, later that year.

As an all-too-obviously eligible bachelor, the young Lord Blandford's name was inevitably linked in the press with that of Princess Margaret, whom he certainly escorted on various occasions. But in 1951 the Princess, together with Queen Elizabeth (now the Queen Mother) and Queen Mary, was among the guests at his marriage to Susan Hornby, whose family own land not far from Blenheim and are associated with the stationers W.H. Smith & Son. There were two children of the marriage.

Both the Duke's elder children are now involved in the Blenheim family business: James, as an apprentice learning the ropes on the estate after a difficult and remorselessly publicized adolescence; and Henrietta (the wife of London banker Nathan Gelber), as an interior decorator recently responsible both for the conversion of the old laundry in the Kitchen Court into the Spencer-Churchill Conference Room and of the old riding school in the stables into the "New Restaurant". James and Henrietta shared one of Blenheim's most memorable recent celebrations (his twenty-first birthday, her "coming-out") on a balmy night in the Jubilee summer of 1977 when 800 guests, including the Prince of Wales (with his then girl-friend and sometime Blenheim shooting companion, Davina Sheffield), Princess Margaret, the Duke of Kent, Prince Michael and the late Lord Mountbatten, danced until dawn in the Library and sat out on the water-terraces amid the fairy-lights. Dazzled by the display of diamonds at the ball, a French guest was overheard to observe: *"Ce n'est plus de la bijouterie, mais de la mineralogie."*

The first married home of James and Henrietta's parents was the usual army "cabbage patch" in Germany, but the shrewd Sunny Blandford had his eye on an ideal property right on the edge of the Blenheim estate, Lee Place at Charlbury. This satisfyingly elegant eighteenth-century building had originally served as the dower-house for Ditchley Park, the next estate down the road from Blenheim. "I was determined to buy it," recalls the present Duke, "but the then owner was unfortunately not interested in selling. However, after she died, one of the Blenheim guides who was conveniently living in the lodge at Lee Place tipped me off that it was coming up for sale and I was able to acquire it, with forty-seven acres, in 1953 after I came out of the army."

Having retired from the Life Guards, Lord Blandford spent a year at the Royal Agricultural College at Cirencester (doing what is known as the "gin and tonic course"), and then settled down at Lee Place to the life of a working farmer on his own account. Initially he rented a farm of 450 acres at Charlbury and then through the 1950s and 1960s gradually took more and more land in hand from the Blenheim estate so that by the time he inherited the dukedom in 1972 he was farming 1,200 acres. This land, the "Settled Estate", then amalgamated with the "Parliamentary Estates" (that is to say basically the park of Blenheim Palace, which had remained under the agricultural sway of his father) to form the Blenheim Farm Partnership.

Lord Blandford's first marriage was dissolved in 1960 on the grounds of his wife's adultery. A year later, in an unruly Greek ceremony in Paris where the milling media-men and women comfortably, or rather uncomfortably, outnumbered the guests, he married Tina Onassis (as she was always billed). The former Athina Livanos had previously been the wife of the famous

Greek shipowner, Aristotle Onassis and, following her divorce from Lord Blandford after ten uneasy years, she went on to marry her brother-in-law, another millionaire Greek of modern mythology, Stavros Niarchos, before dying in 1974. Something of a tragic figure, Tina never became Duchess of Marlborough and is chiefly remembered at Blenheim for her lavish generosity to the staff. Her first Christmas as the Marchioness of Blandford saw expensive handbags being distributed to all the women employed at Blenheim; the following year it rained elaborate Greek handmirrors.

As far as the park was concerned, however, the heir could do little to change what he considered the antiquated agricultural methods, for the 10th Duke's beloved shooting – with its emphasis on plenty of "cover" in the grassland – remained the paramount factor. Before succeeding his father, the present Duke "did his prep" (to use one of his cousin Randolph Churchill's favourite phrases), and bided his time: "I knew what had to be done," he says.

Although the aristocracy has long since lost the last vestiges of its manorial power, its members continue to justify their existence through voluntary service as unpaid rural administrators. The present Duke entered public life as a County Councillor in 1961 (representing Charlbury until 1964) and became Justice of the Peace the following year. He still sits on the magistrates' bench every other week and is a Deputy Lieutenant for Oxfordshire (the Lord-Lieutenant, Sir Ashley Ponsonby, lives close by the Blenheim estate). The Duke holds several presidencies of organizations local to Blenheim, such as those of Oxford United Football Club, the Oxford Association of Boys Clubs (who benefit from the annual charity cricket match played by the ubiquitous Lord's Taverners on the south lawn of the palace), and the Oxfordshire branch of the Soldiers, Sailors and Air Force Association. He is also involved in a number of other charities such as the Sports Aid Foundation, the Forces Help Society and the Lord Roberts Workshops. Local and national organizations have far from given up thinking in terms of ducal leadership; *noblesse* still obliges.

"One disadvantage of living in the country seven days a week is that you get too narrow an outlook – you're inclined to become a potato, if you know what I mean," the Duke says; and he has therefore also taken on various business and public appointments away from Blenheim. "It does me good to go to London, to sharpen my wits with businessmen and so on." He is chairman of his friend Count Rossi's aperitif firm, Martini & Rossi, based at New Zealand House in the Haymarket; and also of London Paperweights which he set up in the mid-1970s. "I met an American who wanted to start a subsidiary," he says. "We actually make and package the paperweights at Blenheim." They prove, needless to say, a popular item in the gift shop.

Opposite: The present Duke at his wedding to his first wife, Susan Hornby, 1951. They were divorced in 1960, having had two children, James and Henrietta.

Upon succeeding to the dukedom in 1972, the Duke took his seat in the House of Lords and delivered his maiden speech during the famous badger debate of February 1973. Championing the cause of this "dear good fellow" (the badger, not the Duke), the late Earl of Arran said there was no evidence that the badger created any significant nuisance. Lord Lovat could think of only three reasons for killing a badger – to make a shaving brush, to make a regimental dress sporran for the Argyll and Sutherland Highlanders or to blood a terrier. The Duke of Marlborough, while agreeing that "the average badger is an attractive and harmless animal", pointed out that "once a badger gets into bad habits he does not give them up". The habits the Duke had in mind were killing chickens and the occasional lamb; he called for an amendment to Lord Arran's Badger Protection Bill to enable landowners to put such badgers down. After the debate he was reported as saying that as far as he knew the badgers at Blenheim "have been decent chaps".

The Duke has also spoken in the Lords about agriculture, the arts and, of course, the "heritage" – that vital new subject which has been so successfully mastered by aristocrats with an instinct for survival. He is President of the Thames and Chilterns Tourist Board (presenting many a plaque to the more successful pubs), of the Oxfordshire branch of the Country Landowners' Association, a body which epitomizes the new business-like approach to landowning, and a member of the council of the Historic Houses Association, the vigorously effective organization which he helped found with Lord Montagu of Beaulieu and others in 1973 to represent the interests of country house owners in the corridors of power. He has campaigned strongly for the abolition of the dreaded Value Added Tax on repairs to historic buildings and takes a particular interest in Heritage Education.

In the spring of 1972, Blenheim not only acquired a new master but also a new *châtelaine*, for in May Countess Rosita Douglas, who comes from a Swedish family of Scottish descent, became the Duke's third wife (and the first to bear the title of Duchess). The new Duchess, a fashion designer and artist, was the daughter of a Swedish ambassador killed *en poste* in Brazil in a motor accident and sister of Her Royal Highness the Duchess in Bavaria. In marked contrast to the previous marriages, this Marlborough wedding was kept as secret and intimate as possible. After an early morning ceremony at Caxton Hall (where Bert, the 10th Duke, had married Laura at the beginning of the year), there was a service of blessing at Charlbury and then a lunch at Blenheim. The staff had merely been told that "a group of Americans" were on their way. The palace's long-serving chief guide, the redoubtable Archie Illingworth, was the only photographer allowed to record the occasion which marked the beginning of a new era at Blenheim.

The decision to move into the "big house" following the death

The Duke is a keen hunter and goes out with the Heythrop regularly.

of the previous proprietor can prove a painful wrench for an heir already well established in an agreeable, private and invariably more convenient home of his own, but it is of vital significance. Once the owner is no longer resident, an historic house dies a little and seldom recovers its momentum or atmosphere. The new Duke of Marlborough and more to the point – for the future of historic houses has rightly been said to depend upon the daughter-in-law – the new Duchess had no intention of being absentees at Blenheim. "We wanted to be here on the spot," says the Duke, "to live above the shop." Both have a genuine feeling of affection and admiration for the palace which was notably lacking in several of their predecessors (Laura, Bert's widow, who always referred to Blenheim as "the Dump", moved out in the summer of 1972). The new Duchess set her heart on creating a family home in the rather austere private wing of the palace which had taken on a melancholy air since the death of the Duke's mother in 1961.

The Duke and Duchess of Marlborough on their wedding day, 1972, in the Italian Garden at Blenheim with his two children by his first marriage.

In the event, it has proved impracticable for the Duke and his new young family to live here all the year round. "It is just 'not on' for young children to grow up without any privacy and there isn't any at the palace during the summer," explains the Duke. Thus a compromise has been worked out whereby the family live at Lee Place from April to September and then move (very much lock, stock and barrel) into the palace for the winter. In the summer months the Duke commutes from Charlbury to his study overlooking the Italian Garden at the palace and his standard duly flies from the tower above the East Gate to show that he is in residence.

Friends of the Marlboroughs point to how much Sunny has blossomed since marrying Rosita. The Duchess, fair, striking, artistic, refreshingly youthful (she is of a younger generation than the Duke) and disarmingly unaffected, describes herself as a *dilettante*. She loves to dabble in her "dirty den" of a studio which is also transported between Blenheim and Lee Place. Drawing on her experience with Ungaro, the Parisian designer, the Duchess set about bringing the private wing at Blenheim to life with new colour schemes, new curtains and masses of new lamps (120 at the last count). "I have a wonderful time fiddling around, putting the materials together to achieve the right effect," she says. "I am an inveterate squirrel and keep on discovering marvellous things in cupboards which I can use and adapt in decoration." The "cold, unlived-in" Smoking-Room has become an invitingly warm family sitting-room (complete with television), in which the great Stubbs tiger and some of the Blenheim tapestries (previously and, in the Duchess's view, dauntingly, displayed in the bedroom next door) are shown off in style. The Duchess's yellow sitting-room has acquired a delicately feminine elegance and the Duke's dressing-room, which leads into his study, has been done over in a suitably masculine, Regency manner.

Since 1973 half-a-dozen rooms on the ground, or rather principal, floor of the private wing have been opened to the public when the Duke and Duchess are not in residence so as, in the words of Paul Duffie, the palace administrator, "to satisfy the curiosity of visitors who want to see how a modern duke lives". The tour, for which special tickets have to be obtained in the Library towards the end of the usual perambulation of the palace, begins at the singularly unimposing doorway in the bowels of Blenheim at the eastern side of the Great Court and then winds its way up the private staircase to take in the rooms *en suite* overlooking the Italian Garden.

The Visitors' Book is on display in the Smoking-Room corridor, always open on the page recording the visit of Edward VIII and Mrs Simpson in 1936; the first entry in this particular book is for Edward VII and the last, I noticed at the time of writing, is for an oil tycoon who owns the *Spectator* – from Albert Edward to Algy Cluff, in fact. The present paying visitor proceeds via the ante-room to the Duchess's sitting-room, and thence through the smoking-room to the bow-windowed dining-room, and principal bedroom to the Duke's dressing-room.

For many visitors to Blenheim this intimate glimpse of the private wing, never permitted in Bert's time, provides a voyeuristic *frisson* which is clearly the climax of their trip. The times I tagged along on a tour conducted by the admirably discreet Marjorie Wells-Cole you could sense that state of rapt attention sometimes experienced in the auditorium during a great theatrical event. One can only admire the modern aristocrat's blithe disregard for conventional privacy in exposing what are known in the heritage trade as their "private parts" in this way; the Duke of Marlborough's colleague in the "Magnificent Seven" (a marketing combination also embracing Beaulieu, Broadlands, Harewood, Warwick Castle and Woburn), the late Lord Howard of Henderskelfe, maintained that privacy is a nineteenth-century taste anyway, and that he would be happy for his customers at Castle Howard to see him sitting on the lavatory (if, of course, they were prepared to pay for the privilege).

The Duchess of Marlborough has also brought a welcome dash of humanity and lightness of touch to the decoration of the State Rooms in the "public" side of the palace, where many of the pictures and objects have been repaired and conserved. She readily admits that she found the task quite overwhelming to begin with:

> Blenheim engulfs you. Although I had been here before, I didn't fully realize what I was taking on. I remember one day driving up to the palace and suddenly saying to myself, "Oh my God what on earth have I let myself in for?" It was all so awesome; beautiful, but breathtaking. I found it difficult to understand how one could make one's own life here when these walls seemed to dictate a certain kind of life of their own. I was scared rigid for about three years until I came to terms with it.

Now she loves it "passionately", but has to guard against being lost in "a cocoon". "It is very easy to vegetate here," she says. "One could shut out the whole world and be blissfully happy."

In reality, the Duchess does nothing of the sort. Apart from running Blenheim, Lee Place and a small house in London (where she and the Duke stay for two nights most weeks), she has recently started her own knitwear and antique business, Rosita Marlborough ("a lot of fun") and is active in various charities, particularly SSNAP. She has worked enthusiastically for this organization, "Support of the Sick Newborn and Parent", in order to raise money to buy equipment for the special baby care unit at the John Radcliffe Hospital, Oxford. The Duchess became involved with SSNAP following the death of her first child, Lord Richard Spencer-Churchill, who was born in August 1973 and remained in hospital care until his death five months later. Tragically, Richard died on Christmas Day, usually the highlight of the Blenheim calendar for all who live and work on the estate.

Christmas at Blenheim is marked by a service in the Chapel on Christmas Eve for people from the estate; and the children's party still flourishes, though the sixty or so attending, including the Duchess's own children, Edward (born 1974) and the boisterous Alexandra (born 1977), now tuck in at the New Restaurant rather than in the Saloon as they did in Duchess Mary's day. Carols are sung to the accompaniment of the Stonesfield Brass Band, a conjuror performs and Bert's old lodge keeper Bill Hollis puts his beard to good use as Father Christmas. The household staff throw their own party on Christmas Eve and the main staff party – all raffles, presentations and jovial good fellowship – comes in the New Year in the riding school (or the

"New Restaurant" as the older hands at Blenheim have to remind themselves to call it). "Christmas at Blenheim is a splendid
tradition," says the Duchess. "We dust down the fairy jewels, get
out the powder blue china and make it a great occasion. The
whole family – including my sisters-in-law and their children
and grandchildren – gather together and we dine in the Saloon
with two roaring fires." Not being entirely familiar with the
stereotyped British yuletide bill of fare, the Duchess initially
planned Christmas menus featuring such dishes as beef stew
and salmon – until a massed Churchillian reproof drummed in
the indispensability of roast turkey.

Blenheim has long held an unusually high reputation for its
cuisine (snobbish gourmets disillusioned elsewhere by ducal
shepherd's pies have been gratified here by creations worthy of
P.G. Wodehouse's Anatole) and the present Marlboroughs enjoy
a mutual interest in good food. Until early in 1985, however, the
culinary artist was not a temperamental Frenchman with a tall
white hat (there are stories of previous Blenheim chefs firing off
air-guns at light-bulbs or rehearsing a knife-throwing act, using
a kitchen-maid as an accomplice, against a still-marked cup-
board), but the friendly, unassuming Liz Jones who came to
Blenheim in 1982 straight from catering college in Stratford-
upon-Avon. "My mother almost fainted when she heard I'd
become head chef at Blenheim aged only twenty," says Liz, who
had a kitchen-maid to help her in the busy winter months at the
palace when there might be sixteen guests for the weekend. In
the summer Liz was mainly based at Lee Place where Kevin, the
footman, helps out with the cleaning and polishing, though she
sometimes cooked lunch at Blenheim for the Duke and Duchess.
Liz Jones retained a healthily detached view of the remnants of
the feudal system at Blenheim and has no time for the tittle-tattle
inherent in such a closed community – a certain (anonymous)
lady guest requiring beer for breakfast, the Duke's passion for
peaches in season and the Duchess's for sorbets were the sum
total of her gossip.

The atmosphere over at Charlbury is, naturally, less formal
than at Blenheim, though even at family lunch in the Lee Place
dining-room, finely lit by tall Venetian windows, ducal traditions are maintained with a butler and a footman in attendance.
At Charlbury, Ray Charoneau, officially the Duke's valet, fills the
role of butler (the Blenheim butler, Patrick Garner, remains at the
palace all the year round) as well as carrying out his normal
duties of satisfying the Duke's soldierly demands for order and
cleanliness. "He's quite pernickety about his clothes and he likes
everything laid out ready for the morning," says the cheerful
Charoneau.

Ray (Christian names at Charlbury, surnames at Blenheim, is
the form), one of the many ex-military men in the Duke's
employ, has been with his perfectionist employer since 1972 and

Above: The Duke and Duchess at the christening of their son, Lord Edward Spencer-Churchill, 1974.

Right: The Long Library decorated for the coming of age of Lord Blandford and the coming-out of Lady Henrietta Spencer-Churchill, 1977.

Opposite: "Oh Brother" (the Duke of Marlborough and Lord Edward Spencer-Churchill up) ready for a day out with the Heythrop.

married Audrey, the family nanny, not long after he arrived. Nanny Marlborough (as she is still sometimes addressed) was originally a childhood friend of the Duke's first wife, Susan, and joined the Lee Place household shortly before the birth of James, to whom she has always been very close. She succeeded Nanny Grassick ("We are a nuisance but we are a necessity," said this Churchillian stalwart of the great British nanny), who harked back to the days when children were seen and not heard.

"When I first came here," recalls Audrey Charoneau, "the children only saw their parents once a day; we had to change them from top to bottom at four o'clock for tea, dress them in frilly petticoats and white buckskin shoes and organdie frocks, just for twenty minutes before the nurserymaid came to clear away." Today, for the second generation, the regime is much more relaxed. Edward and Alexandra lunch downstairs with their parents – though Nanny notes that the children are "slightly more aware of their ancestor's achievements than of their own manners".

The sheer geography of the palace means that life at Blenheim for Edward and Alexandra in the winter months sees their freedom restricted a little more than at Lee Place. But in her determination to create a home in the palace for the family the Duchess has painted the Blenheim nursery with a jolly assortment of butterflies, teddy bears, flowers and Kate Greenaway-style children. In coming to grips with Blenheim, the Duchess says she has been fortunate in having a free hand without a dowager, or whoever, breathing down her neck.

"A battle has been joined between her and Blenheim," wrote the Duchesse de Clermont-Tonnerre about one of Duchess Rosita's predecessors, Gladys Deacon, and this description is, perhaps, still apt. She went on:

> There are days on which the Palace is the victor and triumphs over her; solemn and dignified she takes her walks slowly through the galleries, by the china cabinets, beneath the ancestral portraits, or along the walks of the park, round the lake. At other times, light as an elf, she frisks across the flower-beds, laughs, sheds sunlight on everything and passes with her dog through the court of honour . . . and the palace is annihilated before so much grace and beauty.

The present Duchess's frisking across the flowerbeds is channelled into the flower arrangements at the palace, upon which she has definite ideas: "I love smelly white flowers." Certainly her unstuffy enthusiasm for Blenheim is highly refreshing and has succeeded in winning over the old guard such as Wadman, the 10th Duke's butler. "Your Grace," he told her after she had redecorated the private wing, "I must say that I wasn't at all certain I would like what you were doing to Blenheim, but I have decided that I *do* like it very much."

Wadman still comes out of retirement from time to time to lend a hand to his successor, Patrick Garner whose staff is kept fully stretched in the shooting season when there are often house-parties of up to sixteen guests for a long weekend (from Thursday to Sunday). The day begins for the staff at 7.30 when the rooms are opened; breakfast tends to be taken by the gentlemen guests in the Dining-Room and served to the ladies on trays in their rooms, after which the shooting party will get out at about 9.15. Lunch is taken at a fairly brisk pace at 1.15 and then the table is stripped, cleaned and polished once more in readiness for the more elaborate dinner. Tea is served in the Duchess's sitting-room at 4.30, prompt ("If you miss it, tough luck," says Garner). Drinks follow at 7.30, dinner at 8.15; the ladies' breakfast orders are taken after they have retired to the Duchess's sitting-room and, once the gentlemen have finished their port, breakfast is laid for the morning. It is still an undeniably ducal regimen. "The Duke has adapted to the times in some ways," says Garner, a very diplomatic figure who came to Blenheim in 1980, "but he's been brought up to have things right in a not quite twentieth-century way. If something's not quite right then he'll know it at once. One is always on the *qui vive*, keeping an eye on him. You always want to try and anticipate him."

Garner also keeps a close eye on the visitors paying to visit the private wing. "Security is very tight, though discreet," he says. On one occasion, at four o'clock in the morning, a catering firm clearing up after a function on the public side unwittingly set off the alarms. The butler hastened from his bed to investigate what had happened, but by the time he had reached the front steps of the palace the unfortunate caterers were already being worried by the alsatians of the Oxfordshire constabulary who had responded to the call with commendable speed.

Not all the paying guests on the private side are there for just a few minutes on a conducted tour – some actually come to stay. Like a growing number of historic houses, Blenheim is finding that "PGs" are a necessity; it is made more acceptable by the fact that they tend to be foreign, rich, rather grand and here primarily to shoot. Garner recalls a brace belonging to the dying breed who travel with their own valets. During the shooting season the Marlboroughs might entertain several house-parties of their own friends and guests prepared to pay around £10 to £12 a bird for the privilege of shooting some 500 pheasants on the Blenheim estate.

Although a dedicated shooting man like his father, the present Duke has had to face economic realities and recognize that the sport is no longer a private pastime. The Blenheim shooting has been put on an economic footing with electric brooders and incubators replacing the old broody hens, and more birds being reared, although in these conservation-conscious days the emphasis is now more on a wilder form of shoot. Duck are also a feature of the Blenheim shoot; ingenious hide-aways for the shooters are dotted around the lake. Altogether there are five "beats" at Blenheim, with a beat-keeper living on each, under the supervision of Derek Mundy, the head-gamekeeper, who is also responsible for vermin control on the estate, not to mention poachers.

If the Duchess does not entirely share her husband's love of shooting, hunting is very much a sport in common. They are out with the Heythrop at least once a week, and also hunt with the Beaufort from time to time. The Duke, shod in his father's venerable hunting boots which are virtually only held together by his valet's wax polish (most of which ends up on the saddle and stirrups, to the despair of the grooms), is a rider of considerable daring. The Duchess cuts a stylish figure in her late mother-in-law's elegant habit, even if she cannot quite match her husband's "nerve". She had a bad fall out hunting in 1982 when she was severely concussed, but "thanks to plenty of superglue on the saddle" she is plugging gamely on. The hunters in the stables at Blenheim are immaculately tended by Mrs Boddy and her staff. The tack room, containing Sir Winston Churchill's saddle as a child, old coach equipment and coroneted riding blankets, has a splendidly evocative horsy atmosphere. The Head Groom, Mrs Boddy, seems to enjoy an especially easy relationship with the Duke, openly speaking her mind in the best traditions of equality above and below the Turf. Together, and with her husband, the late Jack Boddy, they have built up the Blenheim Stud into a flourishing concern with five mares.

The Duke had one or two racehorses in conjunction with his mother which were trained by the late Sir Cecil Boyd-Rochfort, and he had some success as an owner at the yard of his old friend and neighbour Jeremy Tree (whose family used to own Ditchley). But in 1981 he decided to start his own stud at Blenheim, tying it in with the agricultural operation. Latterly the Marlborough colours (brown with scarlet hoops, cuffs and cap) have become a familiar sight, thanks to the efforts of the home-bred *Birdwood*, trained by John Dunlop at Arundel on the Duke of Norfolk's estate.

The third of the traditional country sports, fishing, is also to the fore at Blenheim; thirteen boats can be hired for the day, from six in the morning onwards, for coarse fishing on the lake. The view of the fishing craft dotted around Capability Brown's great landscape early on a fine summer morning is one of Blenheim's lesser-known sights. The Duke himself has taken up fishing comparatively recently. He enjoys being alone with his rod on a riverbank, preferably in Scotland or that even more northerly spot, Iceland – or at least "as far away as possible from Blenheim and its problems".

For the Duke, the maintenance of the palace is a responsibility which he takes very seriously, the biggest problem is the vast

Vanbrugh's gilded orb on the palace roof.

expanse of highly porous stone requiring endless attention. "The upkeep of the fabric and the restoration of the roof could be compared to painting the Forth Bridge," says the Duke, "apart from the fact that as we still haven't finished the job we can hardly be said to be starting over again." To photographers who enquire when the scaffolding on the roof might be removed, the Duke replies "Never". A bemused American on the heritage trail stopover between Oxford and Stratford was heard recently observing to his wife about the scaffolding: "Gee, honey, they haven't finished building this place yet."

The restoration of the acres of roofscape began over on the east side of the palace in 1950 and has gradually worked its way round to the west by fits and starts. "The progress entirely depends upon the financial position in a particular year," says the Duke. "We spend every penny we can get." Even with the help of 40 per cent grants from the Historic Buildings Council (now incorporated into the Historic Buildings and Monuments Commission under the chairmanship of Lord Montagu of Beaulieu), the restoration bill must be running at nearly £100,000 a year at the time of writing. The work, which has recently involved the

The Duke presents a trophy to Severiano Ballesteros, winner of the 1980 Golf Tournament sponsored by Martini Rossi of which the Duke is Chairman.

Opposite: The Prince of Wales planting a lime tree in the new Grand Avenue beyond the Column of Victory. The Duke and Bill Murdock, the former agent at Blenheim, are also in the picture.

regilding of Vanbrugh's famous four golden orbs, is being carried out by Oxford building contractors under the supervision of Blenheim's architect Christopher Rayson of Oxford (who succeeded his father). By the end of 1984 it was reckoned that 80 per cent of the roofscape had been restored. Thus the whole operation has to be seen as something in the order of a forty-year job.

Blenheim has its own maintenance staff of a foreman, a plumber, a waterworks man, a joiner, a plasterer/bricklayer, an electrician, a lorry-driver, a labourer, and a part-time joiner, who look after all the general upkeep of the estate and palace on a day-to-day basis. Dick Grieve, the foreman, an electrician by trade, succeeded Jack Hirst in 1981. He reports every morning at 8.30 in the estate office to Mark Venmore-Rowland, the assistant agent, where they settle the day's programme. The urgent jobs to be discussed might include such items as repairing a burst boiler or gas main, a broken pane of glass, an electrical fault, trouble in the pump-house, a blocked lavatory, or general conservation and restoration work on furntiure or around the farm (always a high priority). In a place the size and age of Blenheim Palace something or other goes wrong with remorse-

The Duke, Duchess and the comedian, the late Eric Morecambe, at the annual Lord's Taverners cricket match at Blenheim.

less regularity. Once a week, and then again for special functions, Dick Grieve checks every light bulb in the palace. "Before the last war," he points out, "it cost about £2,500 to heat the palace with coal. Today this amount would barely cover a quarter of the cost of the oil alone, not to mention the gas, electricity and so forth." Invaluable as it is having their own estate maintenance staff, Blenheim has to call in outside firms on a contract basis for the bigger jobs – such as painting, renovations and improvements to the houses on the estate, and the restoration of the palace fabric. The Duke cites the painting of the palace windows as an index of inflation in the terrifying costs of maintaining Blenheim: "In 1961, when I effectively took over the day-to-day management of Blenheim, it cost £4,500; in the early 1970s it had risen to £24,000; now it is approaching £40,000."

Repairs to a large stately home can be a strain on the richest of

The car park at Blenheim is often filled to capacity during the busy summer months.

magnates – even the Duke of Buccleuch with his vast acreages has found difficulties in raising the money to keep a roof over his head – and it has to be remembered that the Marlboroughs, notwithstanding the welcome transfusion of Vanderbilt dollars at the end of the nineteenth century, are comparative paupers in relation to, say, the Grosvenors, Dukes of Westminster. "No yachts, islands, London properties," says the Duke of Marlborough. "Just Blenheim." Contrary to popular belief, opening a house to the public, a condition of receiving a government grant, is hardly ever profitable in itself; in many cases the actual takings from admission fees are not enough to cover the costs of opening. At Blenheim, thanks to efficient management, admission fees, in the words of the Duke, do "cover basic maintenance like lighting and heating – which alone cost well over £50,000 a year – but they don't provide for restoration work, such as the present repair to the south-west tower." However skilfully and energetically places like Blenheim are marketed for "private functions" (potentially much more of an "earner" than the punter through the turnstile), they depend ultimately on the estate, the supporting land without which a big house is doomed.

The Blenheim estate of 11,500 acres is made up of just under 5,500 acres of let land (there are twenty farm tenants with holdings ranging from in excess of 800 acres, though the average tenanted farm is about half that in size); 1,550 acres of woodland and 3,900 acres (including the park of 2,400 acres) are farmed "in hand". The estate holdings are dotted around the park extending from Wootton to the north, Cassington to the south, Charlbury and Fawler to the west and Kidlington to the east. Surprisingly little property in Woodstock, apart from the Bear Hotel, belongs to Blenheim, though one has to remember the Churchills, by squirearchical standards, are comparative newcomers to the area. There are 128 houses or cottages on the estate, of which 35 are let; the rest are either occupied by those directly employed by the estate or the farm partnership, or let with agricultural holdings for farm tenants to house their staff. Over 20 houses or cottages on the estate are occupied by retired estate staff; one of the chief attractions of working at Blenheim is a free house for life (and indeed for the life of your widow).

"An estate like this," says Paul Hutton, the agent who succeeded Bill Murdock in 1978, "is both a source of employment in the countryside and a great influence so far as the quality of the farming and the landscape is concerned. It's because of the concern of the landowners for the land, and their affection for it, that we have the landscape we know today." Hutton, like his celebrated cricketing namesake, is a Yorkshireman and formerly managed the 20,000 acre estate of Viscount Downe at Wykeham Abbey near Scarborough on the Yorkshire Moors. He is not, in fact, an employee of the Duke of Marlborough, but a partner of the chartered surveyors, Smiths Gore, who, as it were, lease him and his deputy, Mark Venmore-Rowland, out on a management contract. The Huttons live in the enviable agent's house, known as China Corner (originally built to exhibit the Spencer-Churchill porcelain collection) near the Triumphal Arch.

The old kitchens, to the left of the Kitchen Court as you enter the East Gate of the palace, house the two agents, a secretary, two accountants, a cashier, a part-time book-keeper, plus another part-timer and could be described as the ganglion of the estate. The atmosphere, however, is agreeably old-fashioned and musty (no computer or evidence of the new technology, one notes with relief). On the wall are maps of the estate, an old photograph of the shooting party for Albert Edward, Prince of Wales at High Lodge, the 9th Duke's triumphant caption to Duchêne's plans for the water terraces (" . . . how I succeeded in destroying the French middle-class view of the formal garden'').

Opposite: View of Vanbrugh's bridge from the air.

View across the water terrace to the west front.

The estate office secretary, Liz Thomas, is a Blenheim institution who brings an affectionate curiosity, perception and skill worthy of her late friend Barbara Pym, the Oxfordshire novelist, to the task of editing the Blenheim newsletter, an occasional publication designed to put everyone on the estate in the picture. Its content, whether issuing friendly warnings to avoid young pheasants or lambs in the park, or reporting on inter-staff cricket matches, or paying eloquent little tributes to retiring retainers

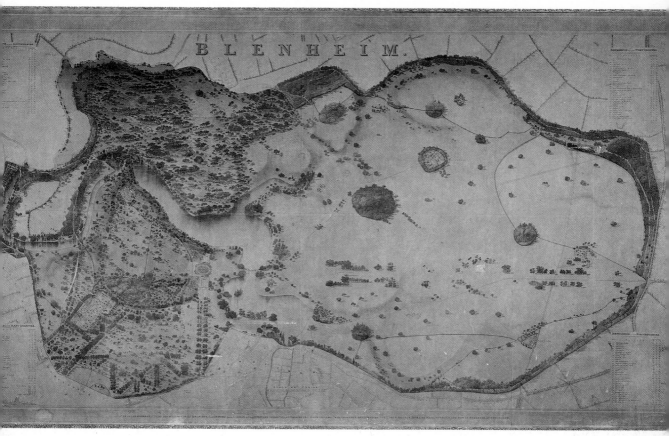

Map of Blenheim Park as it was before Dutch Elm disease ravaged the trees.

("Codge" Simmonds, for instance, remembered an old woman selling glasses of water out of Fair Rosamond's Well at 1*d*. – a tradition soon to be revived through the Blenheim bottling plant being set up in the stables), evokes the flavour of what Bill Parncutt, a former deputy chief guide, nicely describes as "the Blenheim family". Talking to the people around the estate one encounters remarkably little bolshiness. Only a cynic would point to the free housing as the only reason that there are now thirty holders of the long-service tankards that are presented at the staff party to those who have worked for over twenty-five years at Blenheim.

When Jim McVicar, the manager of the Blenheim Farm Partnership, says he has "the finest farm staff in the UK, a multi-skilled bunch who really know their jobs", you are inclined to believe him for this crisp, controlled Scotsman is impressively level-headed. He runs operations from Park Farm, to the left of the Column of Victory as you cross the bridge into the Great Park, with the help of an assistant, a secretary and an Apple computer. The rest of the workforce consists of seven herdsmen, a shepherd, a dairy stock person (female), eight tractor drivers and a couple of agricultural students. McVicar came to Blenheim in the mid-1970s after managing the Lydham estate in Shrop-

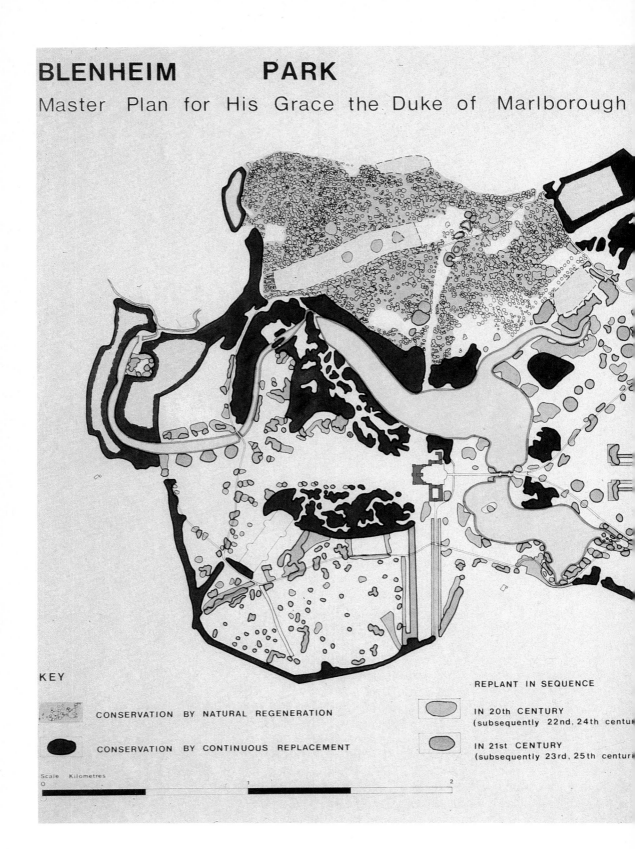

BLENHEIM   PARK

Master Plan for His Grace the Duke of Marlborough

KEY

CONSERVATION BY NATURAL REGENERATION

CONSERVATION BY CONTINUOUS REPLACEMENT

Scale   Kilometres

0   1   2

REPLANT IN SEQUENCE

IN 20th CENTURY
(subsequently 22nd, 24th centu

IN 21st CENTURY
(subsequently 23rd, 25th centur

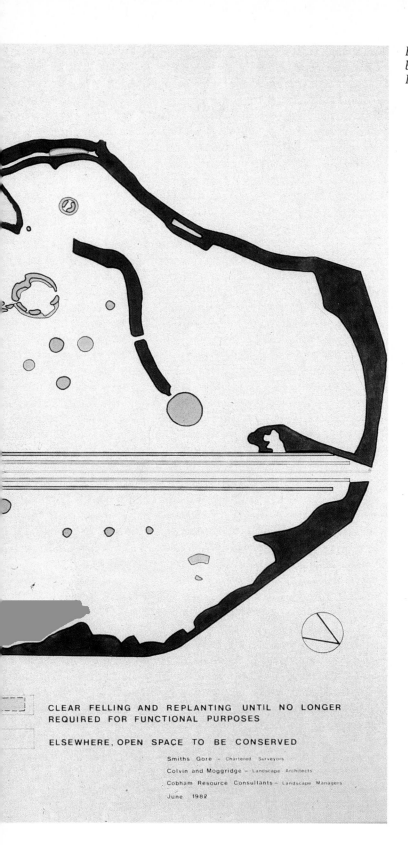

Blenheim Park: as it was and will be . . . The Two Hundred Year Plan.

CLEAR FELLING AND REPLANTING UNTIL NO LONGER REQUIRED FOR FUNCTIONAL PURPOSES

ELSEWHERE, OPEN SPACE TO BE CONSERVED

Smiths Gore – Chartered Surveyors

Colvin and Moggridge – Landscape Architects

Cobham Resource Consultants – Landscape Managers

June 1982

shire for the Sykes family. Although the finances of the Blenheim farming enterprise are kept separate from the rest of the estate's activities and Jim McVicar only has the Duke above him in the "management structure", there is a closely interknit working relationship between the farm manager and the agent, Paul Hutton. Both are phlegmatic, straightforward, unshowy and obviously very able men whose mutual understanding communicates itself in that form of verbal shorthand so indicative of the practical approach they share. The Duke points out that if Blenheim is run like a regiment he is "very lucky in his 'officers'"; he counts himself fortunate in possessing "the ability to pick the right people".

The land farmed "in hand" at Blenheim is made up of a number of individual holdings scattered over a wide area of about a dozen miles (radio telephones are the means of communication), the soil is principally of "Cotswold Brash" though there is also some heavy Oxford clay. The farming policy revolves, in general, around a six-course rotation consisting of two wheat crops, followed by two barley crops, followed by two years "ley". The leys are used mainly by dairy cows (five Friesian herds of about 125 cows each) while the permanent pasture, the bulk of which is parkland, is used mainly by sheep (a flock of 1,100 North Country grey-faced Mule ewes); the 350 or so dairy young stock use both. The breakdown of the 1984 "cropping plan" went like this: 604 acres of winter wheat, 839 acres winter barley, 408 acres spring barley, 144 acres rye or kale, 823 acres leys, 928 acres permanent pasture, 54 acres oil seed-rape and 60 acres of roads and buildings. Prosaic figures, but they literally represent Blenheim's bread and butter in a highly competitive world. The Duke is closely involved in the management of the farming partnership, which is in the names of himself, the Duchess, Lord Blandford and the Trustees, and helps ensure that conservation goes hand in hand with commerce.

A substantial part of the park is designated as a "Site of Special Scientific Interest" by the Nature Conservancy and in recent years, thanks to a grant from the Countryside Commission, an ambitious landscape restoration plan has been put into operation. The 1970s was a disastrous decade for the park: the elms, including those forming the Grand Avenue by the Column of Victory, were devastated by Dutch Elm disease; much of the beech died as a result of the 1976 drought (when Blenheim resembled Arizona); and, in general, the trees in the mature landscape were simply dying of old age. The core of the great work of art, Capability Brown's composition of tree masses and structures set against open lawns and water, had become fragile with age by 1981. This is when the Duke of Marlborough commissioned Cobham Resource Consultants, with the landscape architects Colvin & Moggridge of Lechlade in Gloucestershire, under the guidance of Paul Hutton, to produce both a ten-year

The Duke and Duchess, Lord Blandford and Lady Henrietta (right) at the wedding of Ray and Audrey Charoneau. The bride is the family nanny; the bridegroom, the Duke's valet.

plan and a gloriously optimistic two-hundred-year plan for the future of the park.

The landscape architects categorized the park into eight different zones "distinctive for both historic and functional reasons". The areas furthest from the lake and the palace "will continue to be managed to satisfy modern economic land uses within the setting of historic design features such as the shelter belt which is being renovated". Happily these historic parts of the landscape will keep their distinctive character – for instance, the Great Park is still envisaged as huge in scale and open; the Lince in the south as exquisite and secret; while High Park will remain, in the words of that tireless planter, the 9th Duke, "as an example to all time of the imposing effect of a medieval forest". "They will be a foil to the centrepiece of the park," says Professor Hal Moggridge, "Brown's masterly composition around the

The Duke of Marlborough by La Fontaine.

The Duchess of Marlborough by La Fontaine.

lakes, which is to be restored as exactly as possible as originally planted."

The 200-year cycle is founded on three simple concepts of conservation: natural regeneration in the ancient oakwoods; continuous select felling and replanting of small areas within larger plantations, so that the overall mass is conserved while the trees within them develop a mixed age structure; and replanting whole clumps alternately where groups of trees are too small for continuous select felling. Thus, the 9th Duke's plantations can now alternate with those of Capability Brown in the dry valleys above the lake, resulting in a sequence of historic character over the two-century cycle. The ingenious working out of the vistas from every conceivable angle brings to mind a chart of the scoring strokes all round the wicket by a master batsman.

The Blenheim Forestry Department fields its own cricket team drawn from the twelve foresters working on the woods and the six men at the Combe Estate Yard and Sawmill. Here again, conservation and commerce are carefully combined, under the management of Bob Smith: the constant thinning, clearing, tidying up and replanting in the woods is tied in with the productive business of the mill. Since the elm catastrophe of the mid-1970s, some 700 lime trees have been planted (one of them by the Prince of Wales on a shooting weekend) in four rows over one-and-a-quarter miles in length along the Grand Avenue, while anything up to 30,000 seedlings a year are planted as part of the forestry routine.

Until the mid-1970s Combe Mill, on the edge of the Park, was merely used to supply the palace and the park with its own wood and timber requirements, as well as housing the estate carpenters. Today, the old mill, complete with the recently restored nineteenth-century steam engine, is a flourishing commercial concern with nearly 100,000 cubic feet of timber a year being put through the treatment plant. Estate timber converted into fencing materials, produce from the estate sawmill, and brought-in timber "treated" on contract are supplied to timber and builders' merchants outside the Blenheim ambit — although the estate is still one of the mill's best customers. A current project making use of Combe Mill produce is the Adventure Playground being constructed at the terminus of the small-gauge railway in the Lower Park near the new Butterfly and Plant Centre.

This leisure complex, which succeeds the former Garden Centre, is designed to provide an additional attraction for visiting families. There will be a gift shop, cafeteria and putting course, as well as the Adventure Playground, to complement the chief attraction — up to 150 exotic butterflies free-flying around a great glasshouse that will contain a staple diet of plants growing within. The Plant Centre will sell garden plants and nursery produce from the Blenheim gardens. The gardens — comprising the pleasure-grounds around the palace, the conservatory by the

Italian Garden, the 10th Duke's "private garden" off the south lawn, the nursery unit and the great walled gardens – come under the sway of the estate's head gardener, Andrew Stevenson, who arrived at Blenheim in 1984 after being deputy head gardener to the Queen at Windsor. Altogether he and his staff of 10 (plus a couple of gardeners on the Youth Training Scheme and two or three students in the summer) are responsible for some 100 acres, although out of deference to the landscape comparatively little land is actually cultivated. The soil is alkaline-based and not particularly fertile; rhododendrons, azaleas, orchids and soft fruit are the main features of the Blenheim garden. Sadly, Gladys Deacon's beloved Rock Garden is now completely overgrown and only three of the great glasshouses are left in the nursery (where the new ones seem to have a temporary air), but the old rose garden on the way to the Cascade has been restored recently. Most of the garden produce is sold to wholesalers, although some is retained for the estate. The Duke's favourite melons are carefully planted on a staggered basis so as to ensure a constant supply of fruit from May until September. For decoration in the palace, the Duchess prefers potplants to cut flowers. "The rooms are so ornate," comments Andrew Stevenson, "that plants prove less of a distraction."

Plants such as begonias, geraniums and fuchsias are sold not only in the Centre but in the "Vending Room", part of the Gift Shop complex administered, with a shifting seasonal staff of about ten, by Roy Godwin. A delightfully pessimistic South African, his caustic views on the difficulties of selling books at Blenheim make for salutary listening for stray hacks from Grub Street. There are also sales outlets on the water terraces and in the arcade by the Chapel, while most of the enormous quantity of guide books (one visitor in four to Blenheim buys David Green's masterly work) are sold at the East Gate kiosk.

Here we enter the province of Blenheim's most flamboyant modern character, Paul ("Duke") Duffie. The bow-tied palace administrator is in charge of the opening operation and all its ramifications from the printing of the guide book to litter clearance in the car parks, from public relations to the two launches on the lake, from the gatekeepers to the guides. Duffie began his career as a drummer boy in the Scots Guards and worked his way up to Warrant Officer; running the Officers' Mess gave him highly suitable administrative experience. He is one of the sharp new breed of leisure operatives managing the heritage industry, a Fellow of the Tourism Society, a graduate of the Beaulieu academy of heritage and leisure management and a leading light in the world of tourism. In his time at Blenheim he has pioneered the arrangement of "upmarket private functions" in the palace for the likes of IBM, Ford, General Motors *et al*, and describes his job as securing and selling Blenheim. "My wife and I live in the palace," he says, "and I eat, sleep and think Blenheim."

Overleaf: Two of the private apartments in the east front. The Duchess's sitting-room and bedroom.

*The Duke toasts Archie
Illingworth's health at the Head
Guide's leaving party.*

Duffie's deputy is another ex-Warrant Officer from the Brigade of Guards, Ray Huggins, who was happy to accept the Number Two role, even though he outranks his superior by having been the senior non-commissioned officer in the British army, for "there is only one Blenheim". The Duke unashamedly favours military applications for jobs at the palace ("You know their background and that they will have first-class discipline and loyalty"), which is only appropriate in view of Blenheim's history. The head gatekeeper, David Samuels, and his colleague in the East Gate kiosk, "Taffy" Jones, are both products of the army; both their wives work at the palace and the former's son also works on the estate. There are four gatekeepers, four seasonal helpers about the grounds, four cleaners and up to forty guides employed on a roster basis, together with a secretary, in Duffie's domain.

Duffie arrived at Blenheim soon after the Duke succeeded his father in 1972 and together they have streamlined the opening operation. The number of open days in the season has been increased to seven days a week. A through-flow system in the palace has been arranged by splitting the corridor off the Great

Hall into two, so as to avoid traffic jams caused by people coming in and out of the Churchill Exhibition (opened in his centenary year, 1974, by his widow, Baroness Spencer-Churchill). The optional guided tours have been phased so as to provide more space for those who want to wander along on their own.

The survey information tabulated on the visitors to Blenheim has a certain interest (though Duffie is the first to agree that it does not always have a practical use): 53 per cent of the visitors are from Britain, 24 per cent from the USA; 75 per cent come by car, 23 per cent by coach (feet and bicycles account for the balance); 60 per cent come from within a fifty-mile radius; 35 per cent stay for less than two hours ("Stratford next stop . . ."), 52 per cent for up to four hours; 54 per cent avail themselves of the catering facilities; just under 50 per cent buy something, at least, in the Gift Shop; under 1 per cent travel on the small-gauge railway; 99.625 per cent find the staff "efficient and polite"; lavatories are marked at 8 out of 10; the grounds and gardens are the most liked feature with "no preference" coming close second and the Churchill Exhibition third; 14 per cent are on their second visit. The "most disliked feature" yielded an incoherent

Archie Illingworth hands over the coroneted front-door key to his successor, Paul Duffie.

Left: The smoking-room in the private
apartments. The tiger is by Stubbs.
Above: The Duke's dressing-room.

241

crop of contradictory verdicts and 72 per cent can think of nothing to complain about at all. The comments can occasionally be diverting; back in the nineteenth century Jennie Jerome tagged along on a guided tour, only to overhear one of her compatriots exclaim before a family group: "My, what poppy eyes these Churchills have got!" One Blenheim guide recalls an entry in a Comments Book: "Guides too old and too ugly; should be done away with," but the overwhelming majority are extremely favourable ("The guides make history live", etc.).

The more important statistics, the overall visiting figures, have

Barry Manilow in the Great Court at Blenheim before his concert in the park, 1983.

improved again recently after the general slump in tourism at the end of the 1970s. Apart from 361,547 people who paid to see inside the palace in 1984 (an increase of nearly 6 per cent on the previous year), thus putting Blenheim comfortably into the top twenty most-visited historic buildings in Britain, at least another 100,000 come into the park which is open every day of the year. Special events attract yet more visitors: the Blenheim calendar includes the Churchill Memorial Concert in March, the Woodstock Horse Show and Lord's Taverners cricket match around Whitsun, as well as memorable one-offs like the RAC Rally in

Overleaf (left): Lady Alexandra Spencer-Churchill learning to ride a bicycle, with the Duchess in pursuit.
Right: The Marlboroughs at home with their children, Edward and Alexandra.

1980 and the Tory rally for Mrs Thatcher in 1977. In 1983 40,000 fans of Mr Barry Manilow thrilled to an open-air performance by the Brooklyn warbler in the Bladon end of the park ("as far away from the house as possible," in the Duke's words). If the Duke did not go quite so far as his "Magnificent Seven" colleague Lord Tavistock (who described the similar Neil Diamond show at Woburn as one of the most important events in the history of that stately home), it was nevertheless generally agreed to have been a memorable evening, with Mr Manilow (né Pincus) wiggling his buttocks to general hysteria.

Blenheim has continued to be a popular location for film-makers and, thanks to the "Brideshead" contract perfected by another of the "Magnificent Seven" owners, the late Lord Howard of Henderskelfe, such deals are now highly lucrative for historic houses. Recent films featuring Blenheim have included *The Scarlet Pimpernel* and *Greystoke*, as well as the Churchillian television series *Jennie* (with Lee Remick as Winston's mother and the then chef's infant daughter as the youthful hero) and *The Wilderness Years* (with Robert Hardy, now apparently destined to play WSC in a musical, *Winnie*). Mel Brooks caused something of a sensation at Blenheim when filming his *History of the World, Part I* in which he played a *garçon de pisse* touring the grounds (supposed to be representing Versailles in the eighteenth century) with a bucket in order to allow the gardeners to relieve themselves. "Sunny told me they never had this kind of service in England," quipped Brooks. "They were afraid that a careless attendant might have killed the flowers."

Setting aside the showbiz razzamatazz – and what Alan Bennett has described in his classic play *Forty Years On* as a "sergeant's world" where "spare time is leisure" – it is encouraging to see the emphasis placed at Blenheim on education, for that is where the true value of "heritage" lies. To his great credit, the Duke of Marlborough set up the Blenheim Heritage Education scheme in 1979. Harold Fawcus, a retired prep school head-master, the palace's first schools liaison officer, co-ordinates the visits of over 15,000 schoolchildren every year from some 300 different schools. The school parties tend to come early, before the palace officially opens at eleven o'clock, and can use the specially converted schoolroom in the stables as well as a picnic hut in the park when they are on the Blenheim Nature Trail. Heritage education covers the complete life of a country estate; the Blenheim school kits include notes on the park, gardens, forestry, ornithology, sawmill and farms as well as on the mili-tary, social and architectural history. Blenheim received one of the Sandford Awards for Heritage Education in 1983 from Lord Sandford, President of the Council for Environmental Education, for its excellent educational facilities. The Duke of Marlborough himself presents annual prizes for the best pieces of work carried out as a result of visits to Blenheim.

The Duke and Mrs Thatcher at the 1977 Conservative Rally held at Blenheim.

The problem for Blenheim, and for other popular showplaces, is that more means worse. Often the "heritage" industry inadvertently spoils what it sets out to preserve. Too many visitors not only adversely affect the aesthetic atmosphere (for part of the thrill of these places is rediscovering a secret Garden of Eden), but also, eventually, destroy the very fabric through remorseless wear and tear. Paul Duffie wonders if a sort of Disneyland-style "viewing-tube" (that is to say, a hermetically sealed passage suspended in mid-air through the palace) can be far away.

Whatever happens, the Duke and Duchess of Marlborough are determined "to keep Blenheim going". The Duke feels "an enormous pride in Marlborough and what he did for Europe, and I consider it of prime importance that such a supreme part of our heritage should be maintained. My task is to ensure that my heir finds the palace in the best possible state of repair and the estate in good order." Although the Duke has not yet won the present Battle for Blenheim (externally, at least, much remains to be done), he has certainly taken the fight into the modern age, using the most efficient men and weapons he can command in a way his great ancestor would surely have approved.

Above: The Duke setting off for a day's sport.   *Right: "Number 11", wired for sound.*

Acknowledgements

The author would like to thank the Duke and Duchess of Marlborough for their encouragement, advice, practical help and hospitality during the preparation of this book and for access to the Blenheim archives. Special thanks are also due to Paul Hutton and his staff in the Estate Office; and to Paul Duffie and his staff in the Administration department at the Palace. Among the many other people in and around Blenheim who kindly rendered valuable assistance were: Mrs Jack Boddy, Ray and Audrey Charoneau, Mr and Mrs Bob Deacon, Harold Fawcus, Patrick Garner, Roy Godwin, Dick Grieve, Jack Hirst, Mr and Mrs Bill Hollis, Phon Hollis, Ray Huggins, Archie Illingworth, Sid Jakeman, Liz Jones, Taffy Jones, Helen Leslie-Carter, Jim McVicar, Derek Mundy, Bill Murdock, Tom Page, David Samuels, Bob Smith, Andrew Stevenson, Harry Stockford, Liz Thomas, Mark Venmore-Rowland, Ted Wadman and Caroline White.

The author would also like to thank Laura Duchess of Marlborough for her kindness and hospitality; Mrs Edward Phillips for letting him see the papers in her possession concerning the 8th Duke of Marlborough's romance with Lady Aylesford; and Hugo Vickers who generously made available the source material for his admirable biography *Gladys, Duchess of Marlborough* and was a constant source of help, advice and hospitality, way beyond the calls of friendship. Christina Oxenberg was a splendidly skilful and stylish researcher on the project; and among others due acknowledgement are Gillon Aitken, Mark Bence-Jones, Alastair Forbes, Mary Killen, John Montgomery-Massingberd and Carole Winlaw.

Finally, the author must thank Julian Shuckburgh of Shuckburgh Reynolds for inviting him to write this book and for his great patience and forbearance; Gila Falkus, for so expertly editing and improving the text, and for seeing the book through the press; Jenny de Gex, the picture researcher; and Barney Blackley and David Machin of the Bodley Head for their sympathetic support.

Select Bibliography

DAVID GREEN

David Green, the supreme authority on Blenheim, deserves a bibliography to himself. The author, like anyone writing on this or related subjects, obviously owes Mr Green an immense debt of gratitude for his masterly studies based on many years of original research among the Blenheim Papers (now in the British Library). It would have been tedious for the reader if the text of this book had incorporated even a fraction of the references due to Mr Green's scholarship ("as David Green has pointed out..." could easily have become an endless refrain), and their absence should not be taken as indicating any lack of respect on the author's behalf for this great expert.

Apart from Mr Green's guidebooks to *Blenheim Palace* and *Blenheim Park and Gardens*, his principal works of relevance have been: *Battle of Blenheim* (1974); *Blenheim Palace* (1951); *Gardener to Queen Anne* (1956); *Grinling Gibbons* (1964); *Queen Anne* (1970); *Sarah Duchess of Marlborough* (1967); *Sir Winston Churchill at Blenheim Palace* (1959); and *The Churchills of Blenheim* (1984).

OTHER SOURCES

Asquith, Lady Cynthia: *Diaries 1915-18* (1968)
Balsan, Consuelo Vanderbilt: *The Glitter and the Gold* (1953)
Barnett, Correlli: *Marlborough* (1974)
Battiscombe, Georgina: *The Spencers of Althorp* (1984)
Birkenhead, Earl of: *The Life of F.E. Smith, 1st Earl of Birkenhead* (1960)
——*The Prof in Two Worlds* (1961)
Blakiston, Georgiana: *Woburn and the Russells* (1980)
Buckle, Richard (ed.): *Self Portrait with Friends: Selected Diaries of Cecil Beaton 1926-74* (1979)
Burnet, Bishop: *History of My Own Times* (1724-34)
Carnarvon, Earl of: *No Regrets* (1976)
Channon, Sir Henry: *Chips*, diaries ed. by Robert Rhodes James (1967)
Churchill, Randolph: *Sir Winston Churchill* (Volume I, 1968)
—— *Twenty-One Years* (1964)
Churchill, Lady Randolph: *Reminiscences* (1908)
Churchill, Peregrine, and Mitchell, Julian: *Jennie* (1974)
Churchill, Sir Winston: *Marlborough: His Life and Times* (1947)
—— *Lord Randolph Churchill* (1906)
Colvin, H.M.: *A Biographical Dictionary of British Architects 1600-1840* (1978)
—— *The History of the King's Works*
Complete Peerage, ed. by "G.E.C." et al (1910-59, 13 vols).
Coward, Noel: *Diaries*, ed. by Graham Payn and Sheridan Morley (1982)
Cowles, Virginia: *The Great Marlborough and his Duchess* (1983)
Coxe, W.C.: *Memoirs of John Duke of Marlborough* (1820)
Dictionary of National Biography
Downes, Kerry: *Hawksmoor* (1979)
—— *Vanbrugh* (1979)
Gronow, Captain Rees Howell: *Reminiscences and Recollections 1810-60* (1900)
Harris, John: *Sir William Chambers* (1970)
Holroyd, Michael: *Lytton Strachey*, 2 vols (London 1967/8)
Lees-Milne, James: *Ancestral Voices* (1975)

—— *Prophesying Peace* (1977)
Leslie, Anita: *Edwardians in Love* (1972)
—— *The Gilt and the Gingerbread* (1981)
Leslie, Shane: *Long Shadows* (1966)
Marlborough, Laura Duchess of: *Laughter from a Cloud* (1980)
Martin, Ralph G.: *Lady Randolph Churchill*, 2 vols (1971/2)
Mavor, Dr W.F.: *New Description of Blenheim* (1787-1846)
Reid, Stuart: *John and Sarah, Duke and Duchess of Marlborough* (1914)
Rowse, A.L: *The Early Churchills* (1969)
—— *The Later Churchills* (1971)
St Aubyn, Giles: *Edward VII* (1979)
Soames, Mary: *Clementine Churchill* (1975)
Stroud, Dorothy: *Capability Brown* (1975)
Vickers, Hugo: *Gladys Duchess of Marlborough* (1979)
Walpole, Horace: *Letters* and *Journals* (various editions)
Whistler, Laurence: *Sir John Vanbrugh* (1938)
—— *The Imagination of Vanbrugh* (1954)
Ziegler, Philip: *Lady Diana Cooper* (1981)

Picture Sources

Index